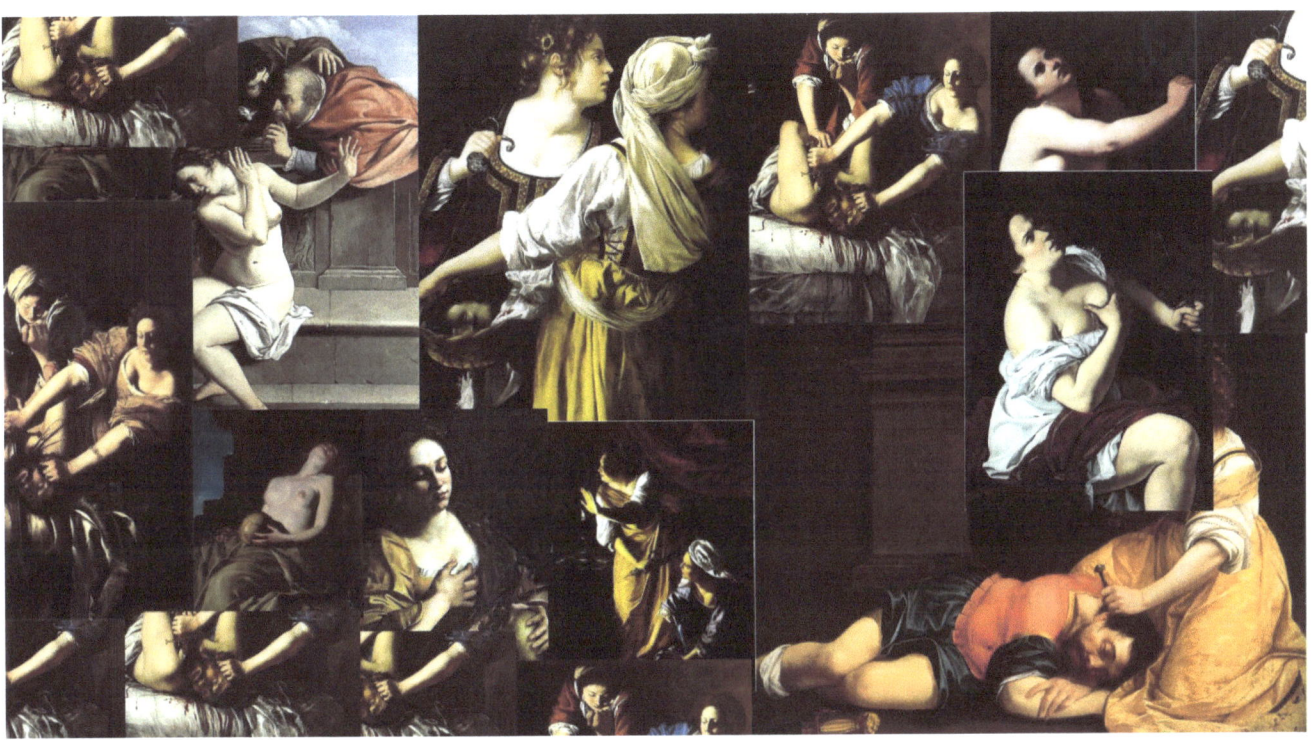

Artemisia Gentileschi

Edited by Linda Savage

Artemisia Gentileschi was an Italian Baroque painter born in Rome, Italy in 1593 and in Naples, Italy in 1656.

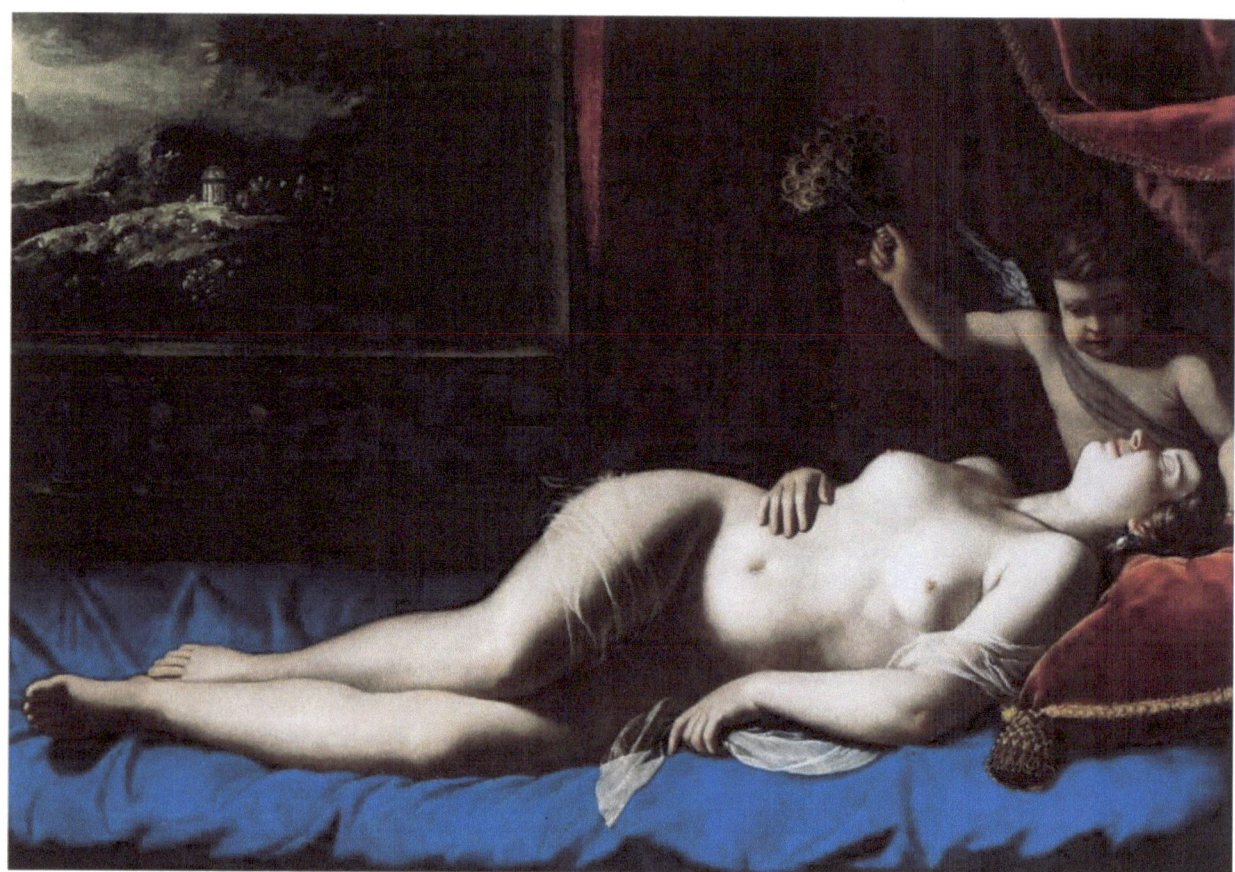

Sleeping Venus-- Artemisia Gentileschi –1630--Baroque

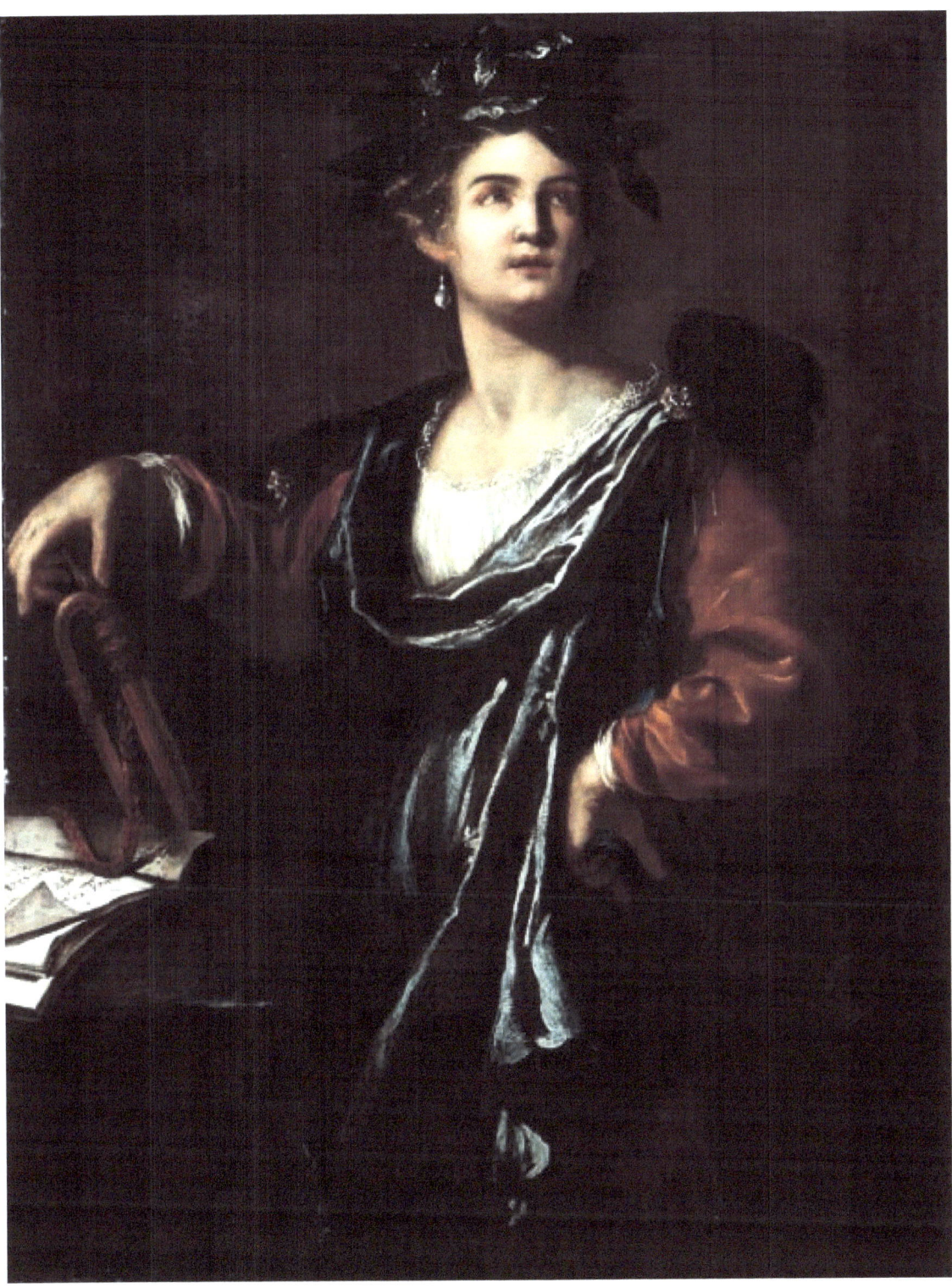

Clio, the Muse of History--1632

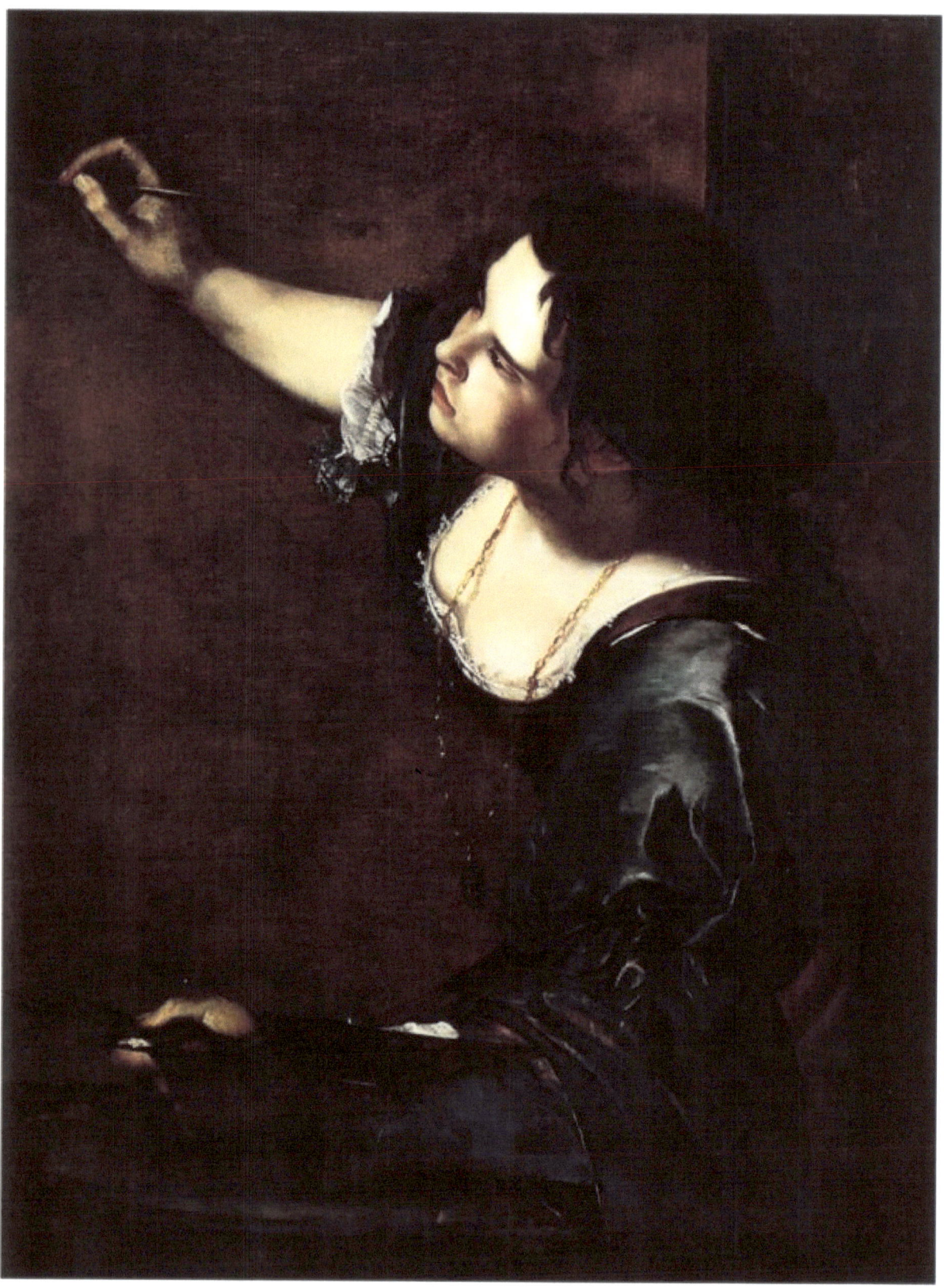

Self-portrait as the Allegory of Painting—1639--Baroque

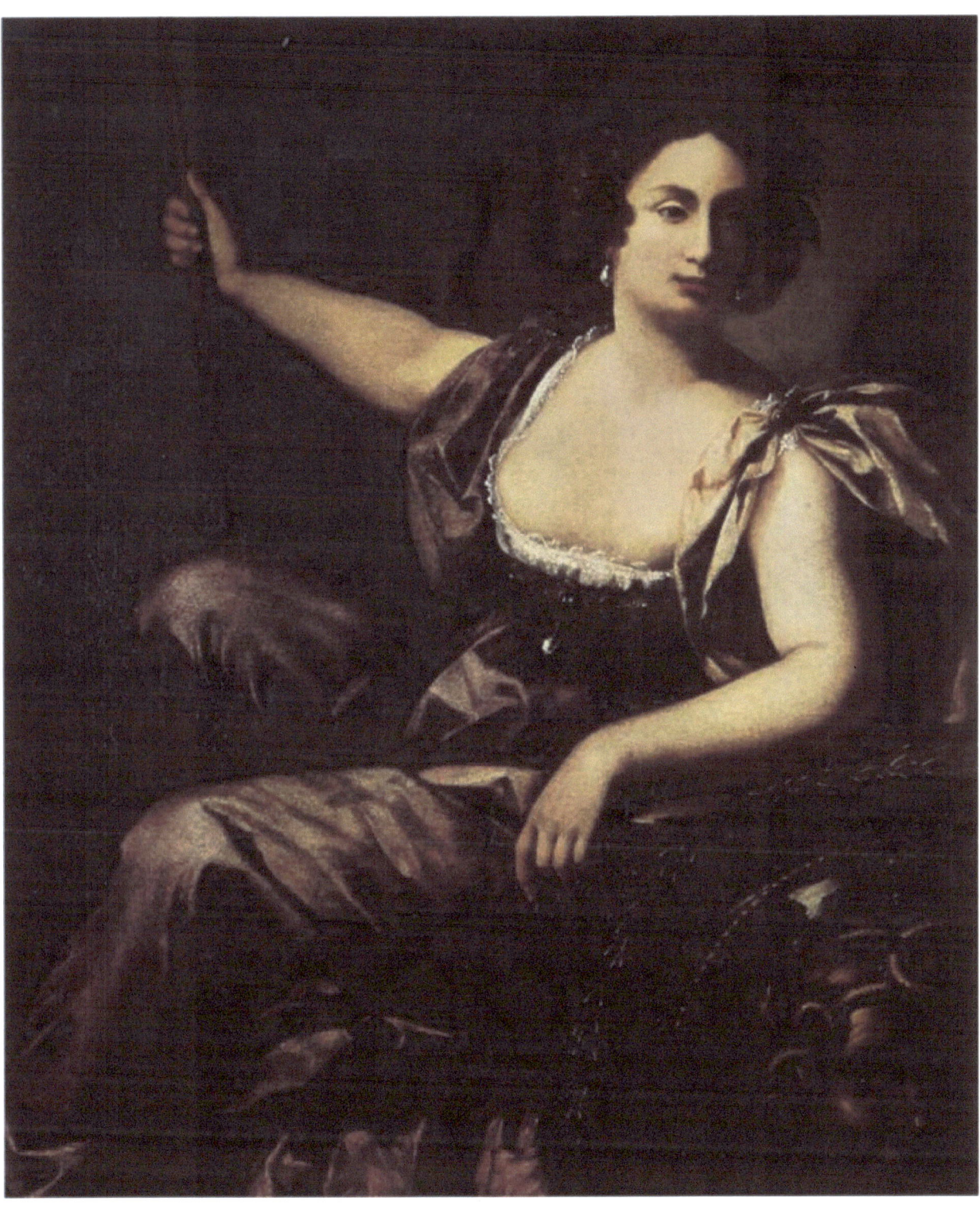

Minerva—1640-- Baroque

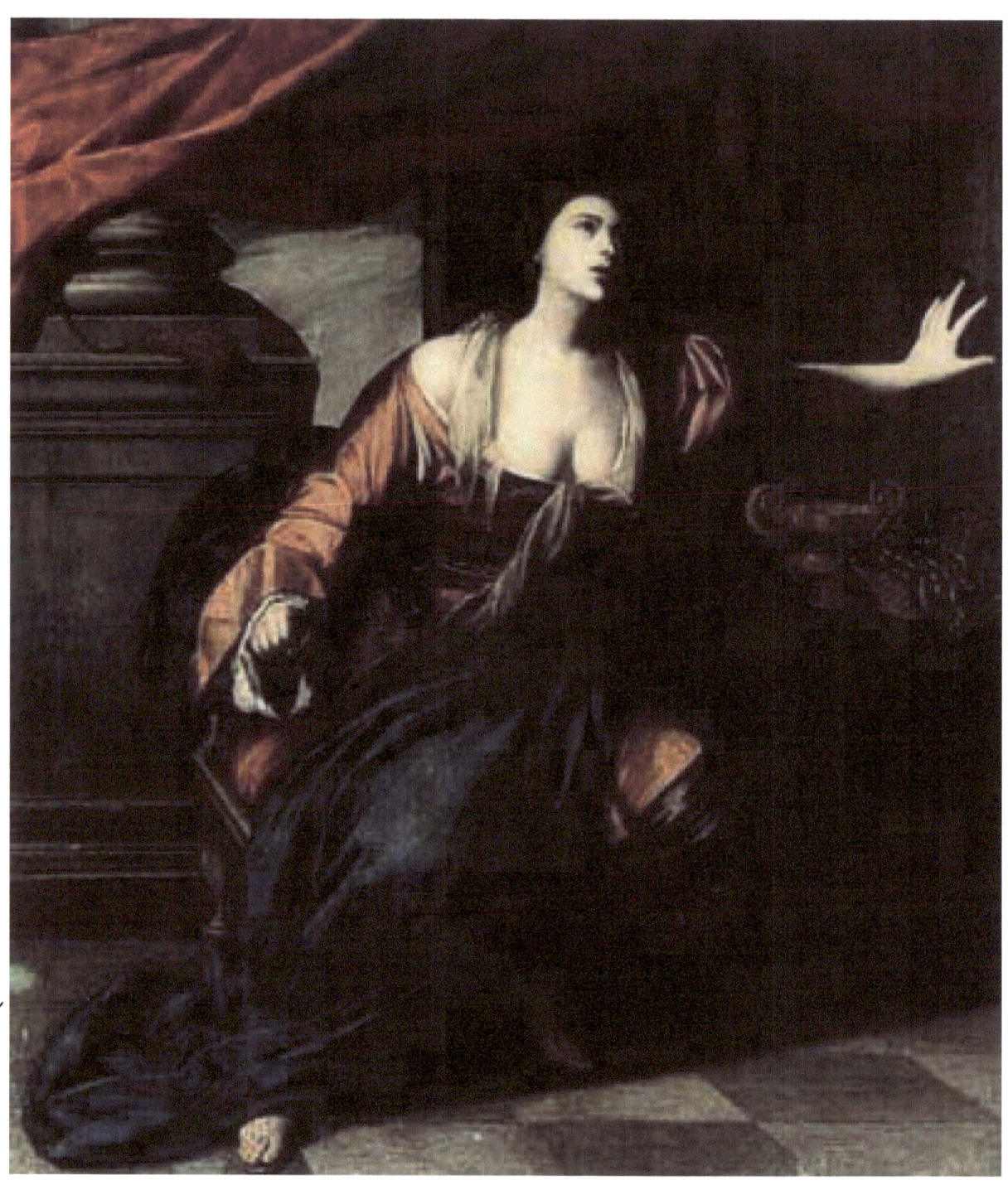

Lucretia —1642--Baroque

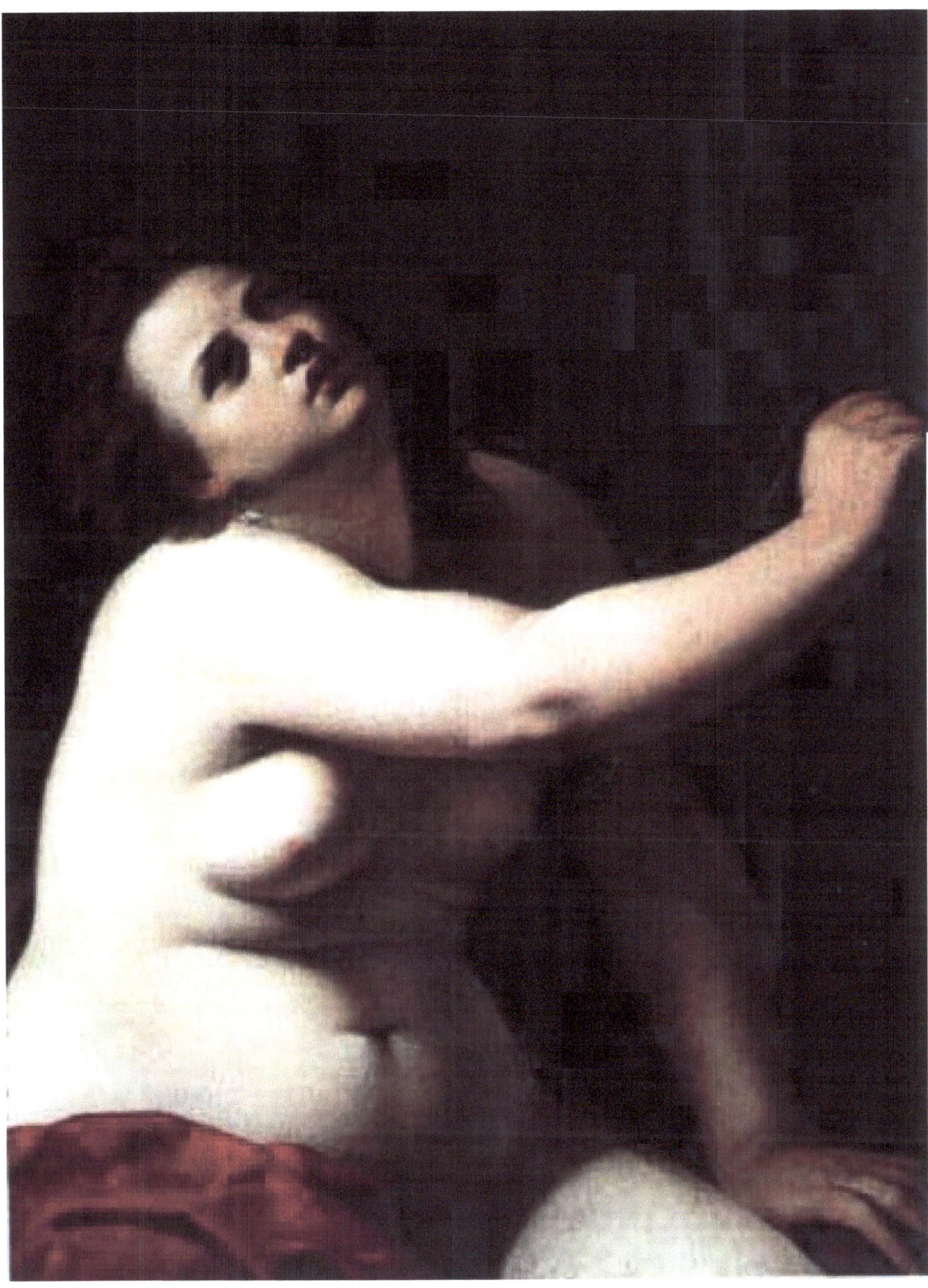

Cleopatra--Baroque

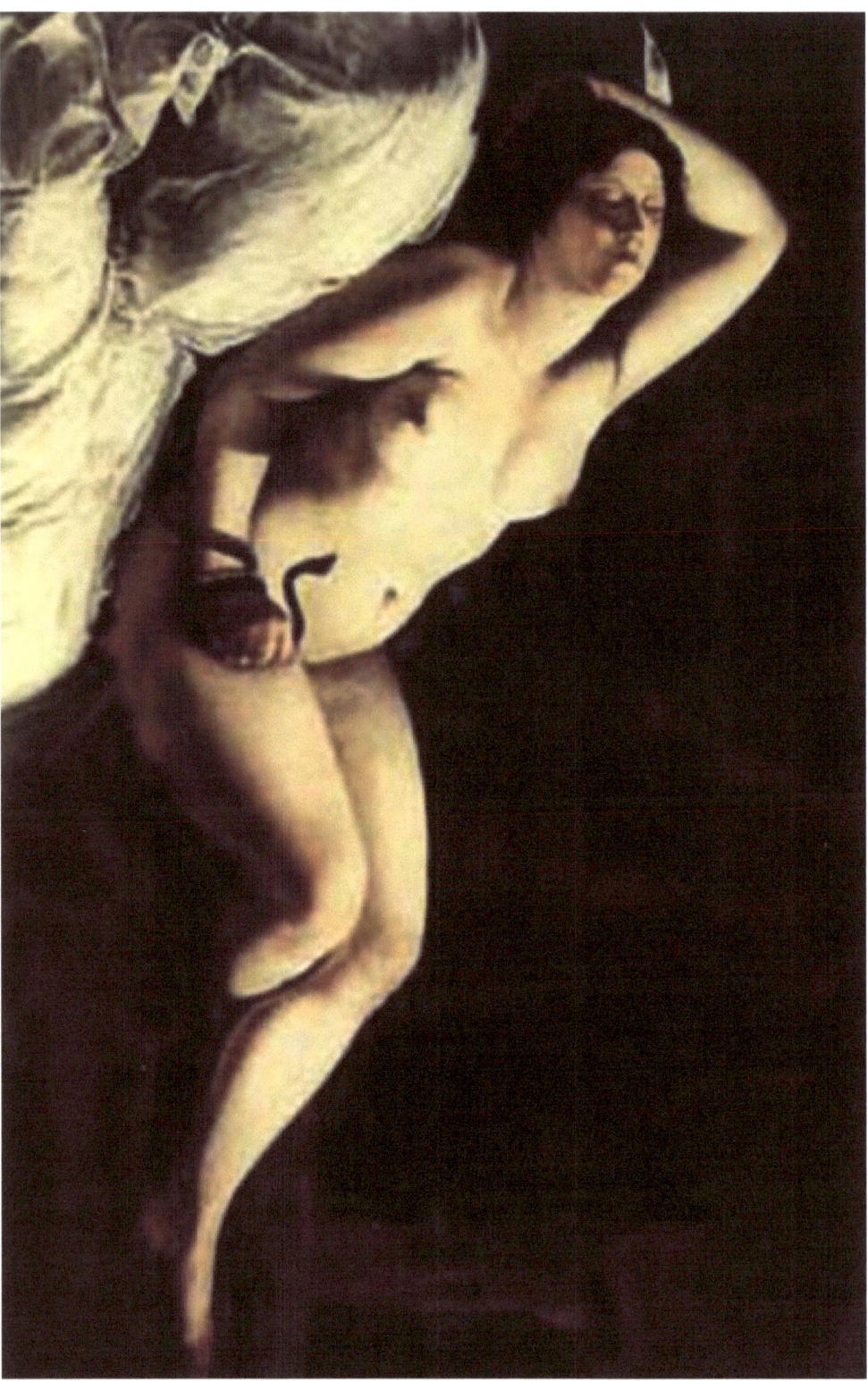

Cleopatra--Artemisia Gentileschi(?)

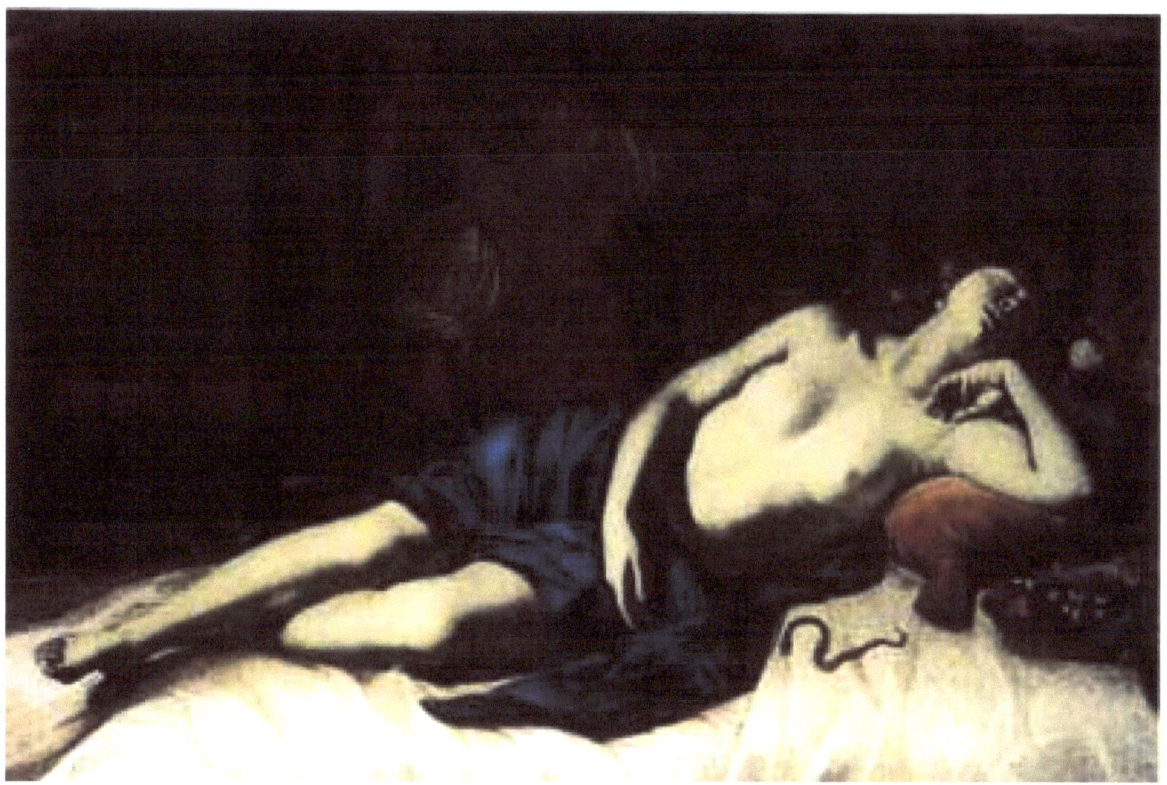

Cleopatra--Artemisia Gentileschi(?)

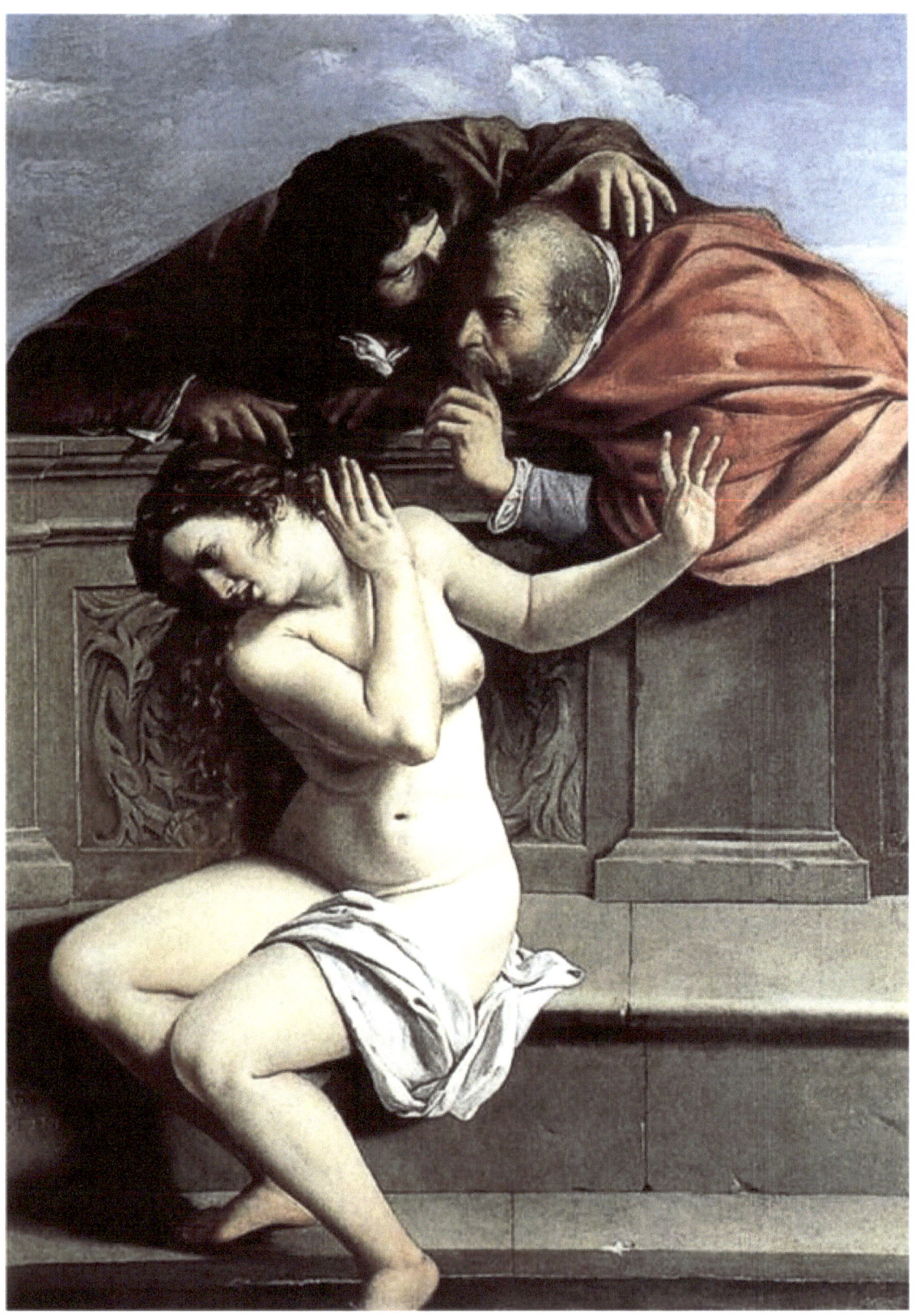

Susanna and the Elders—1610-- Baroque

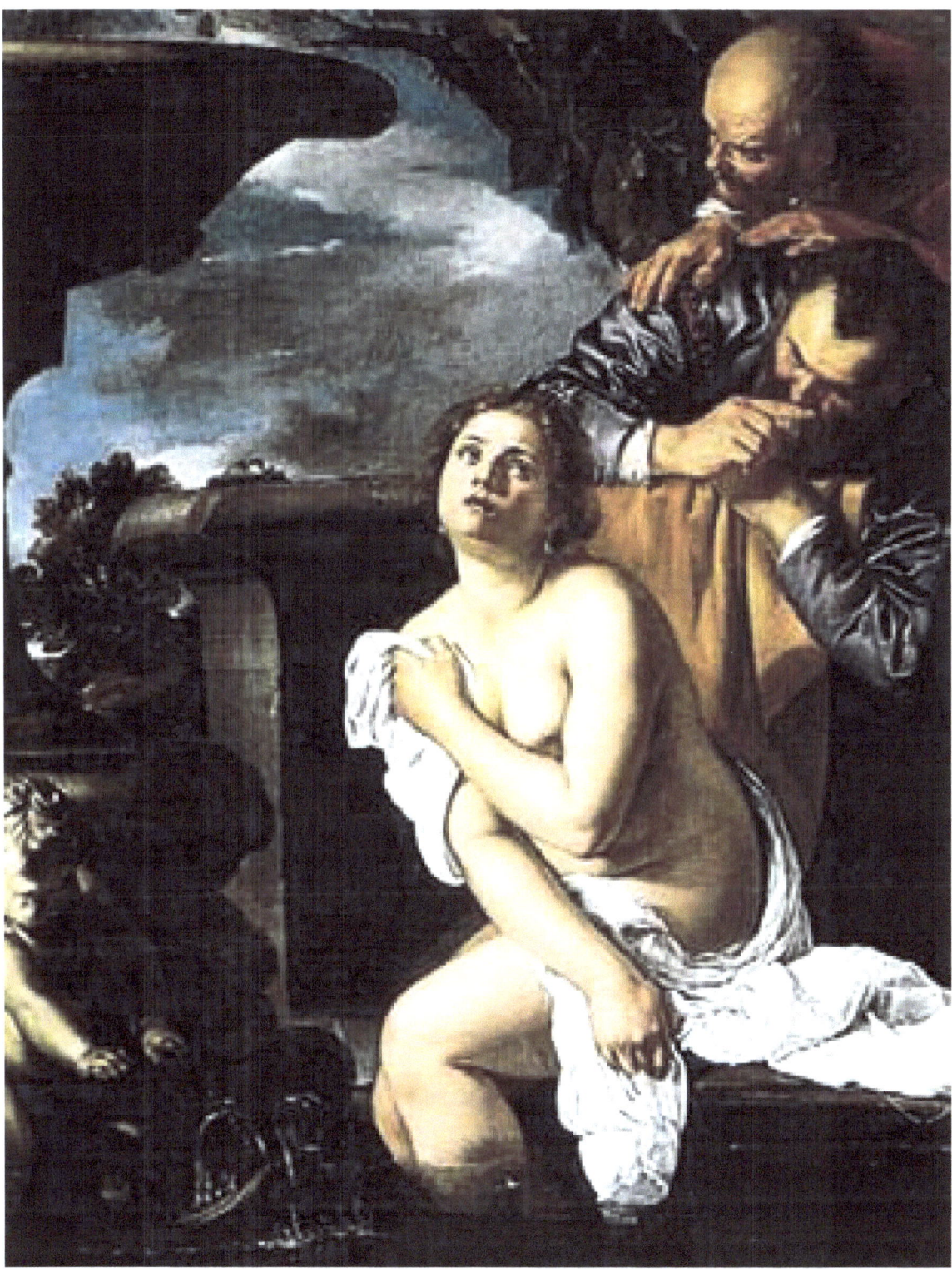

Susanna and the Elders—1622--Artemisia Gentileschi(?)

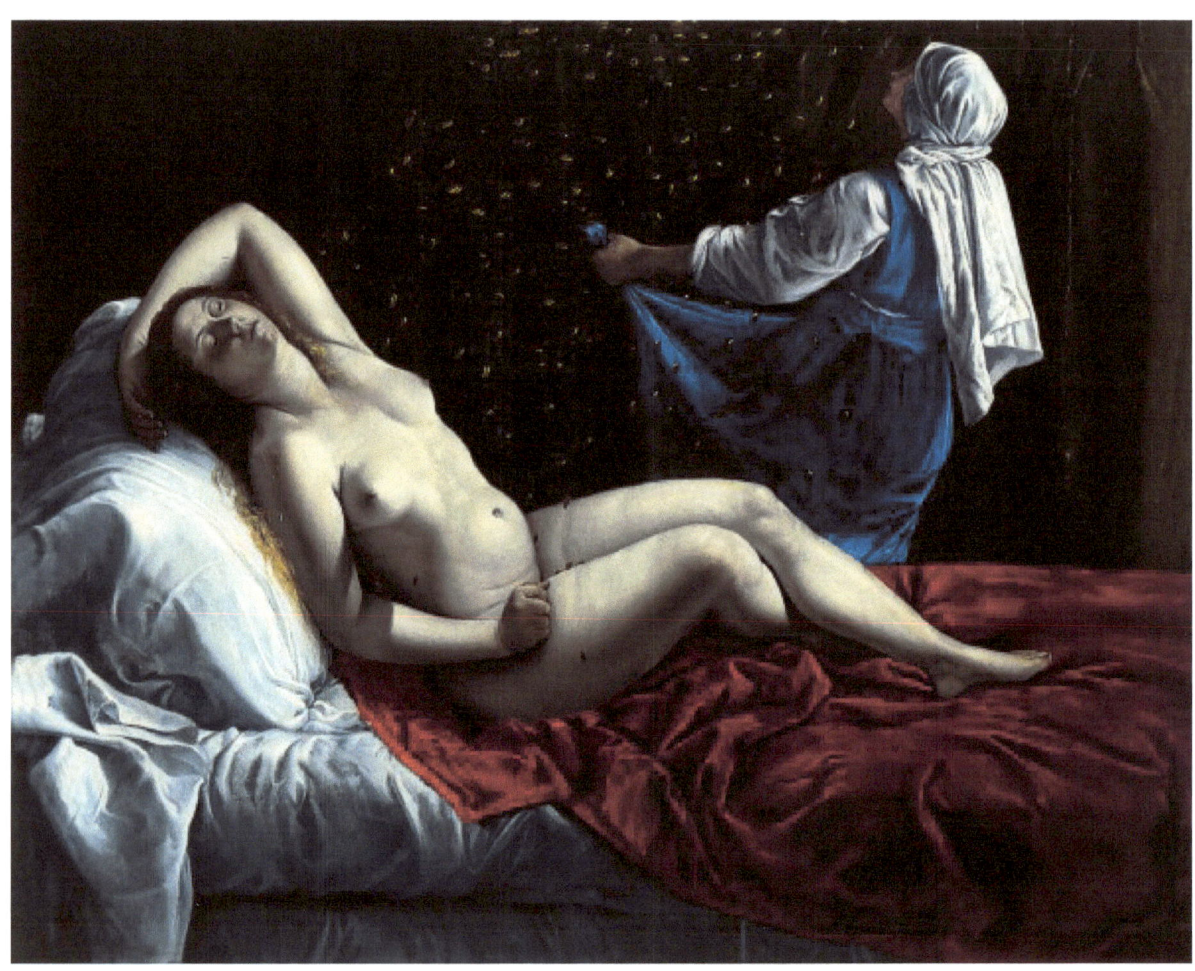

Danae—1612--Baroque

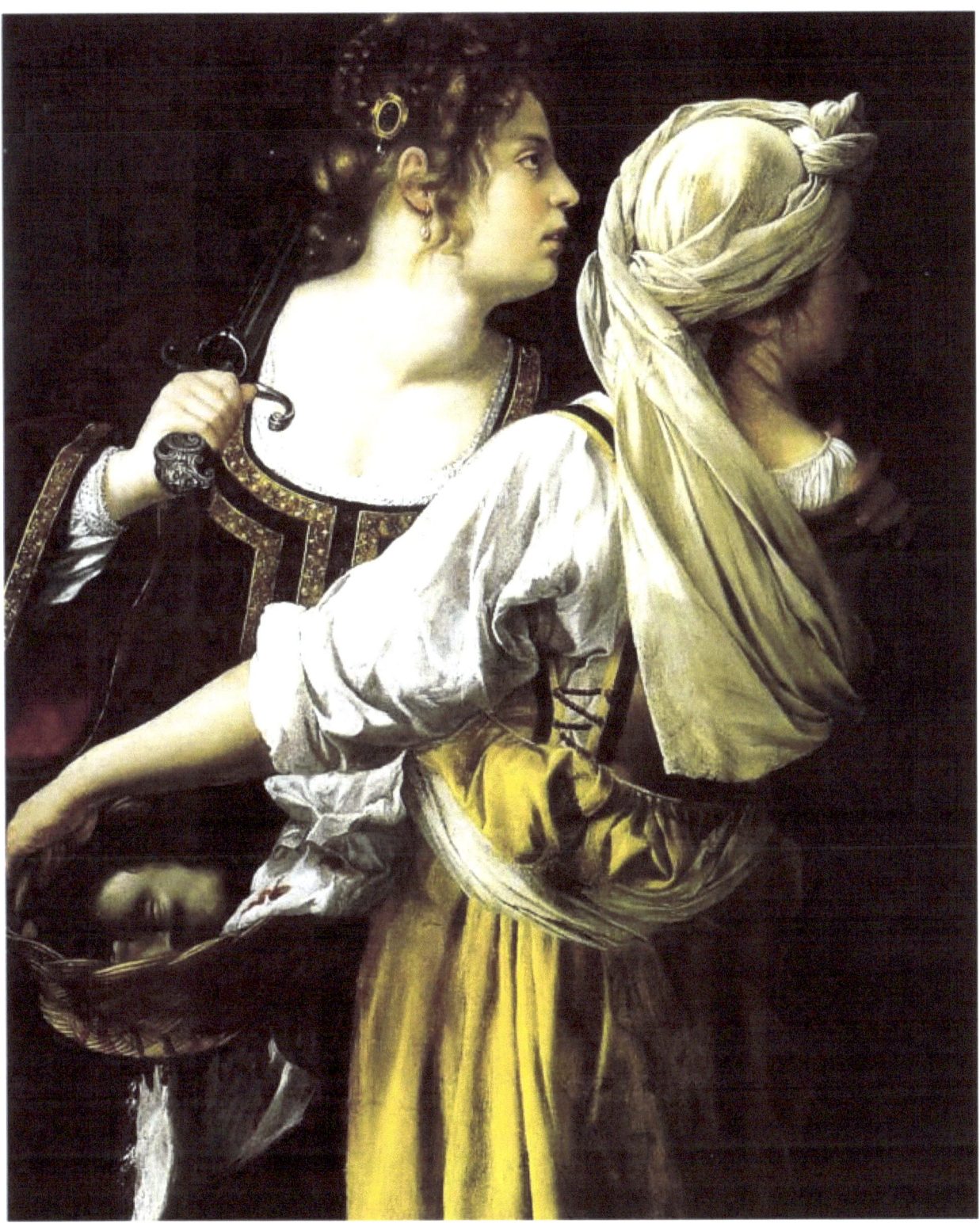

Judith and her Maidservant –1613--Baroque

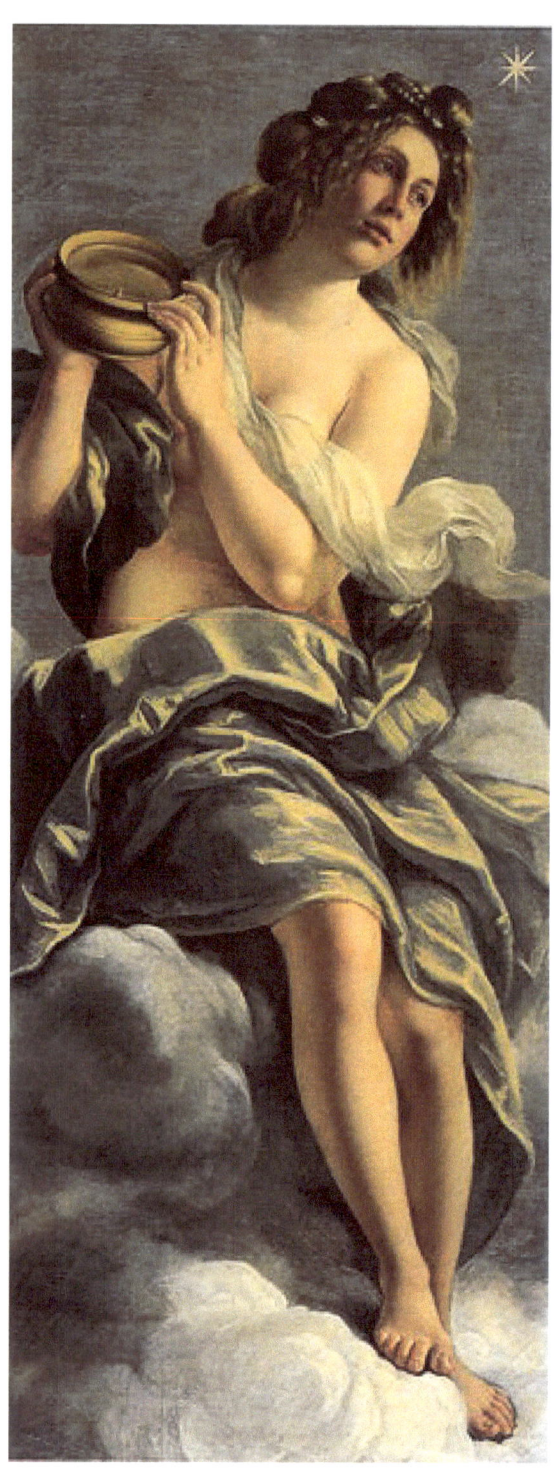

Allegory of the inclination (The Angel)—1615--Baroque

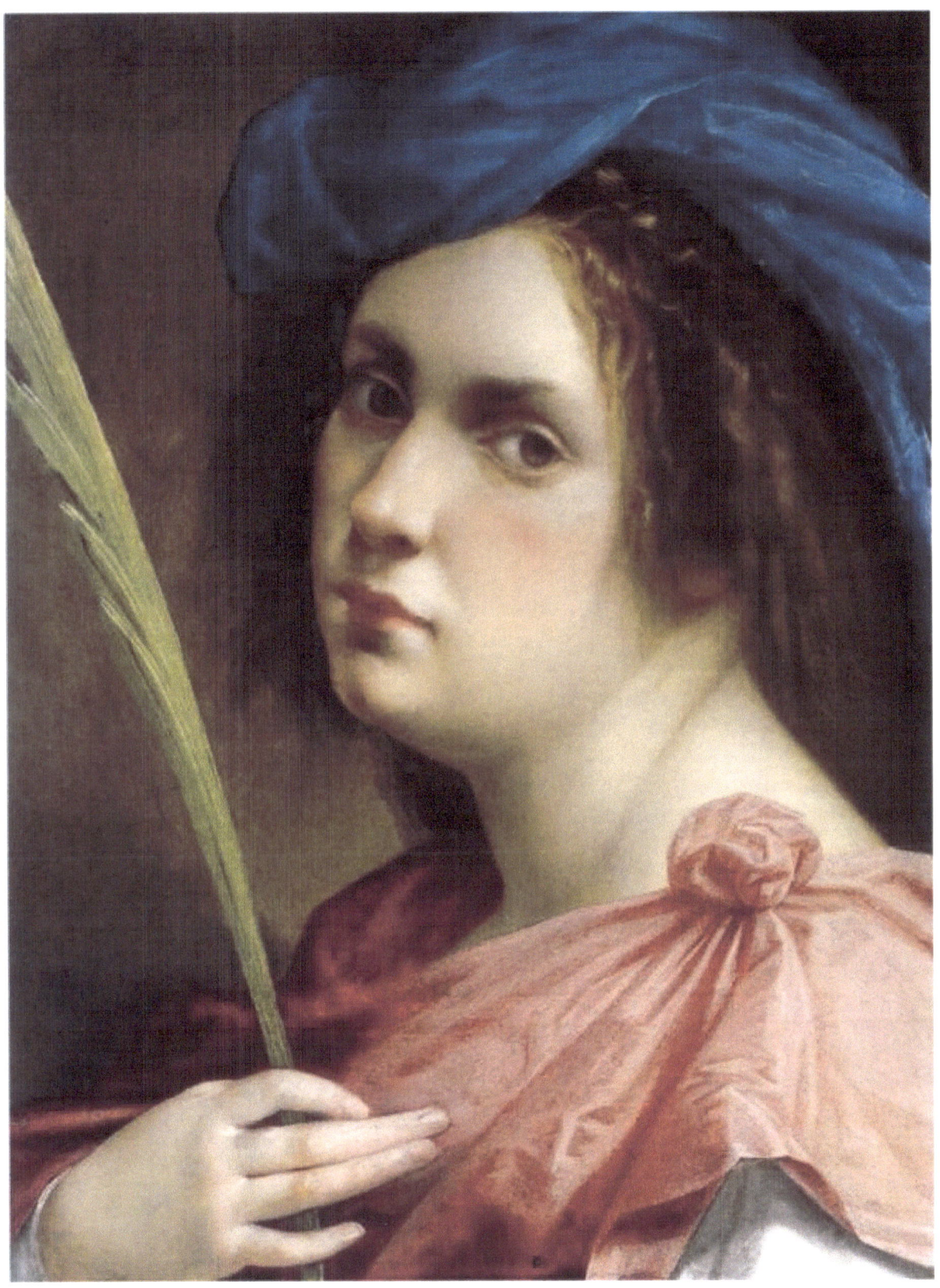

Self-portrait as a Female Martyr—1615--Baroque

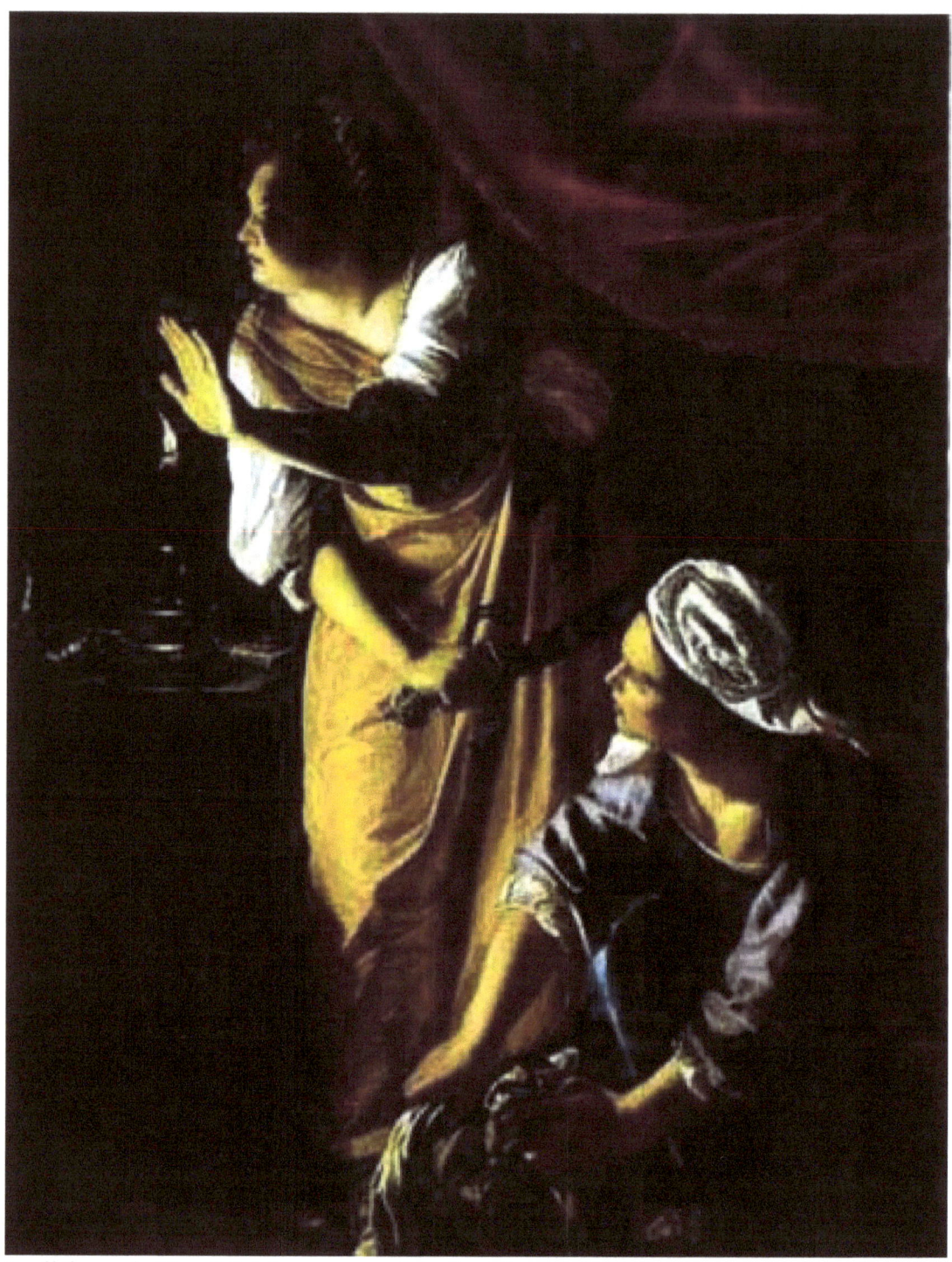

Judith and Her Maidservant with the Head of Holofernes--1625

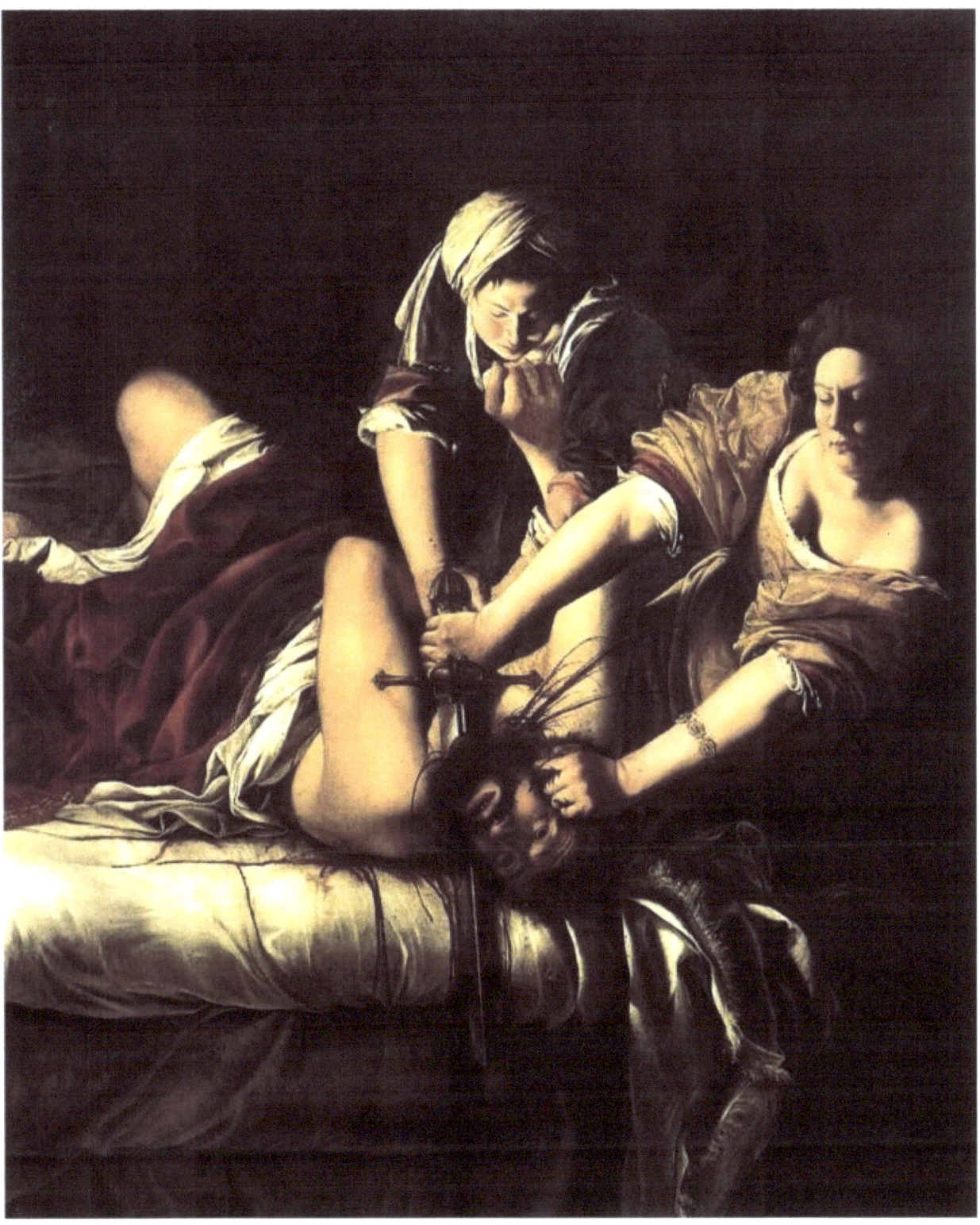

Judith Beheading Holofernes—1620--Baroque

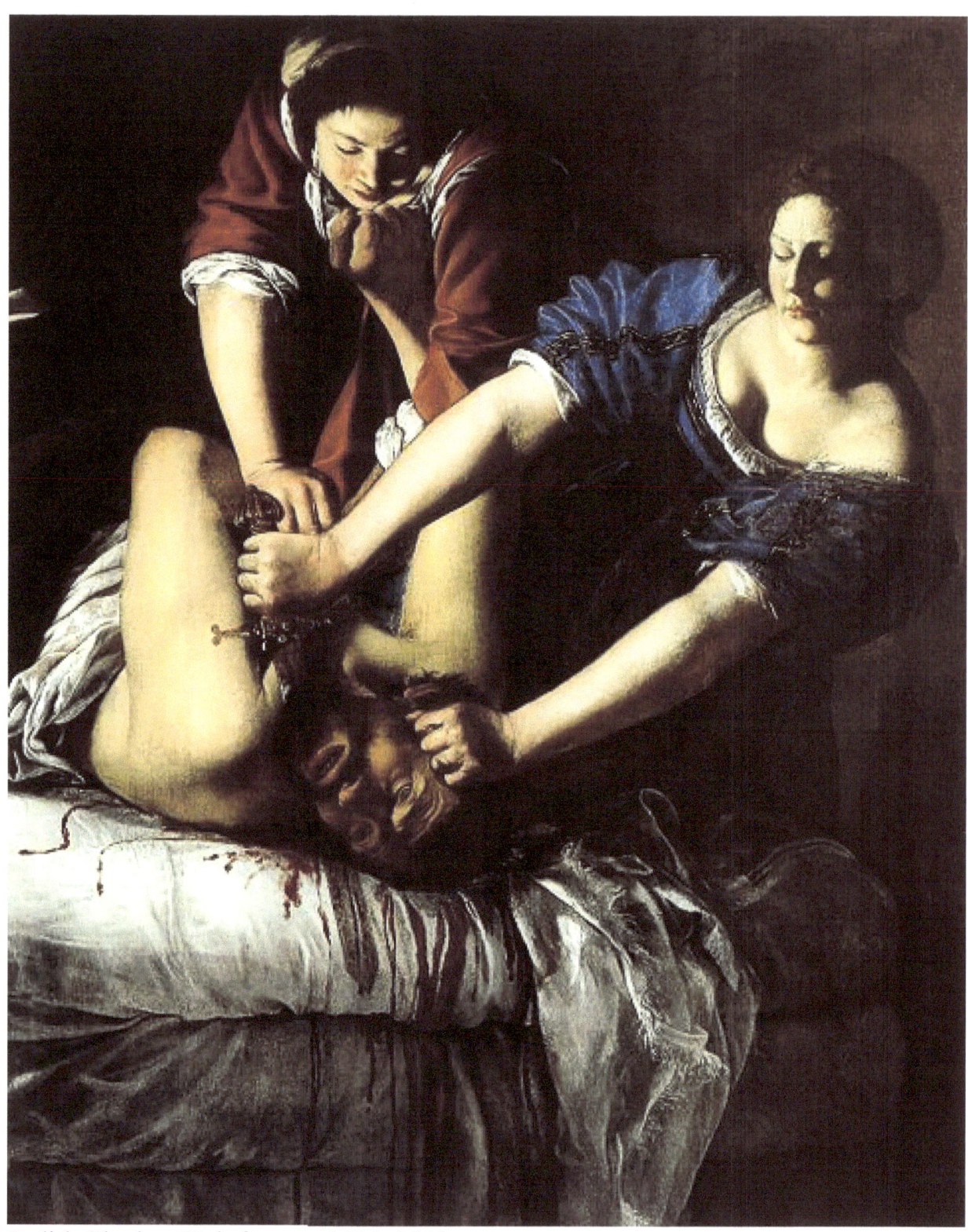

Judith Slaying Holofernes--1612-1613

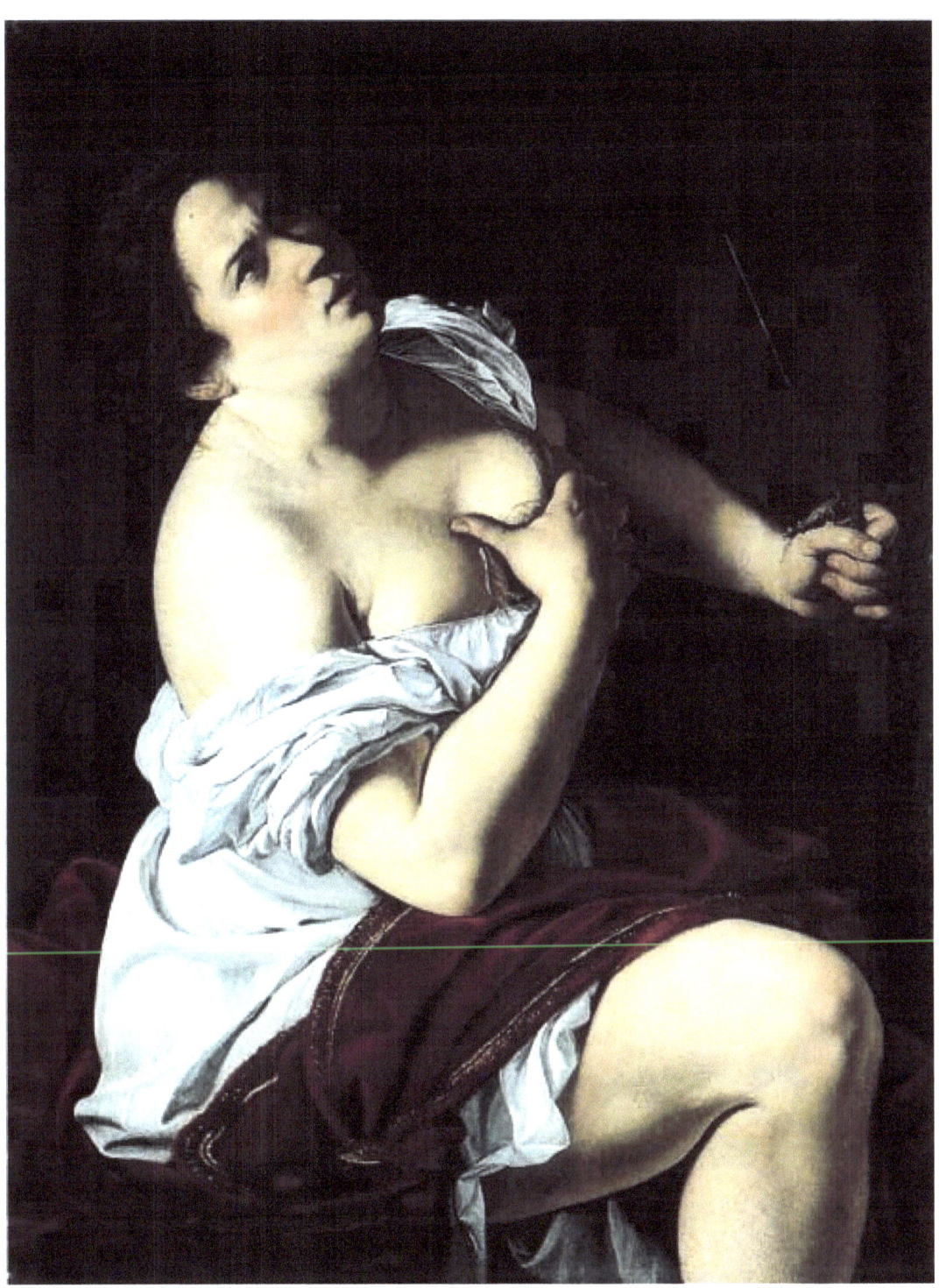

Lucretia—1620--Baroque

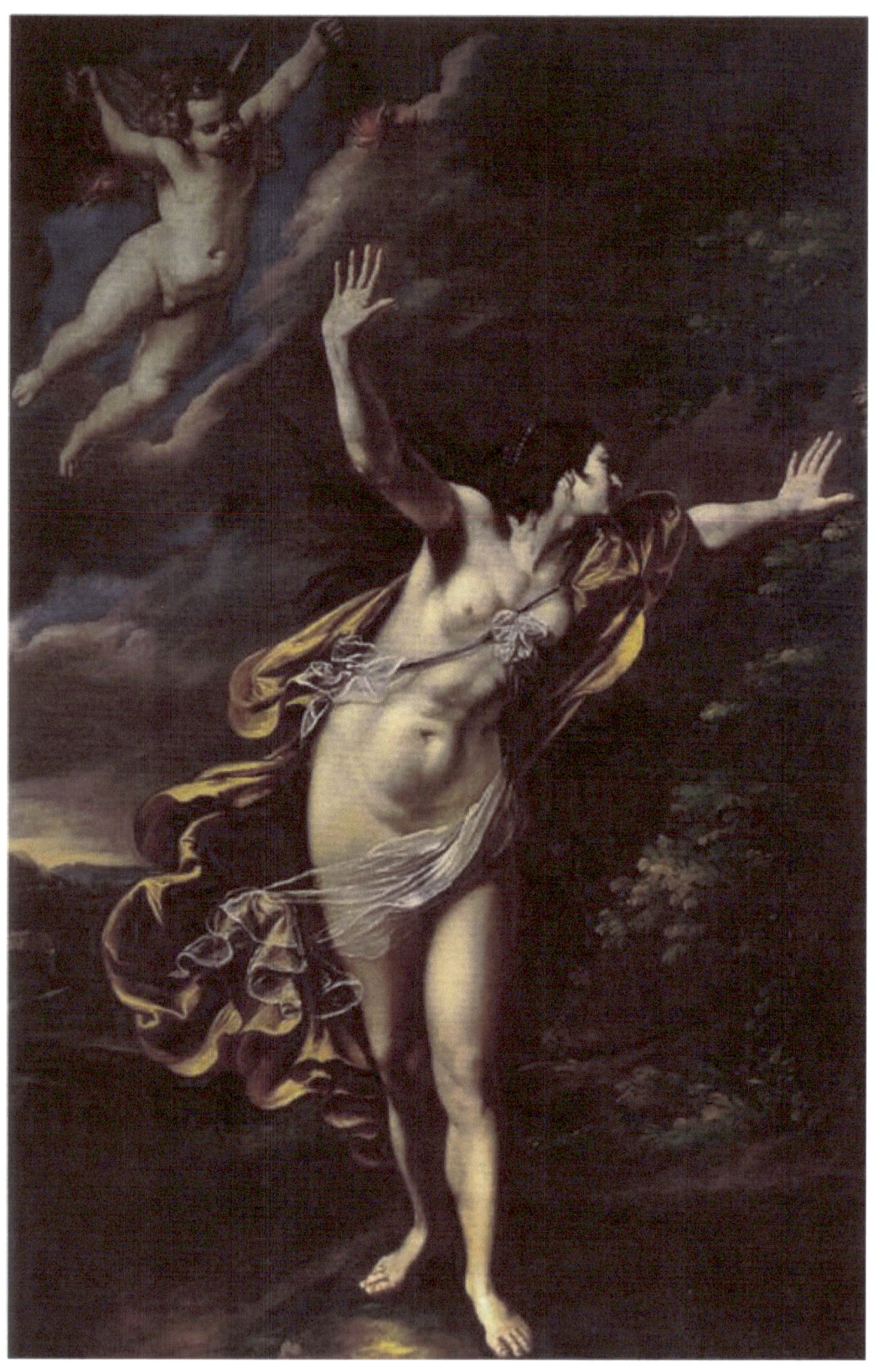

Aurora –1627--Baroque

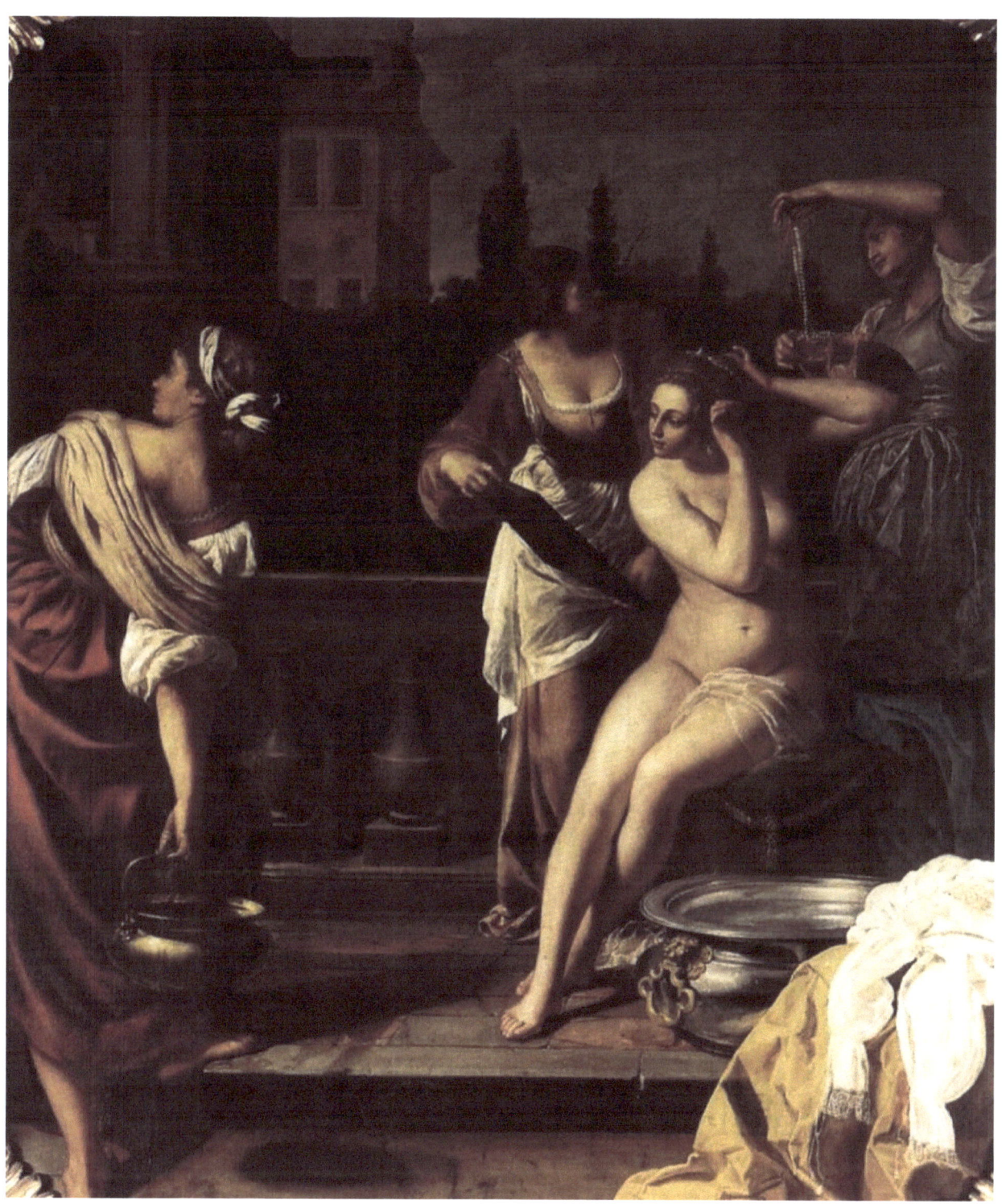

Bathing Bathsheba

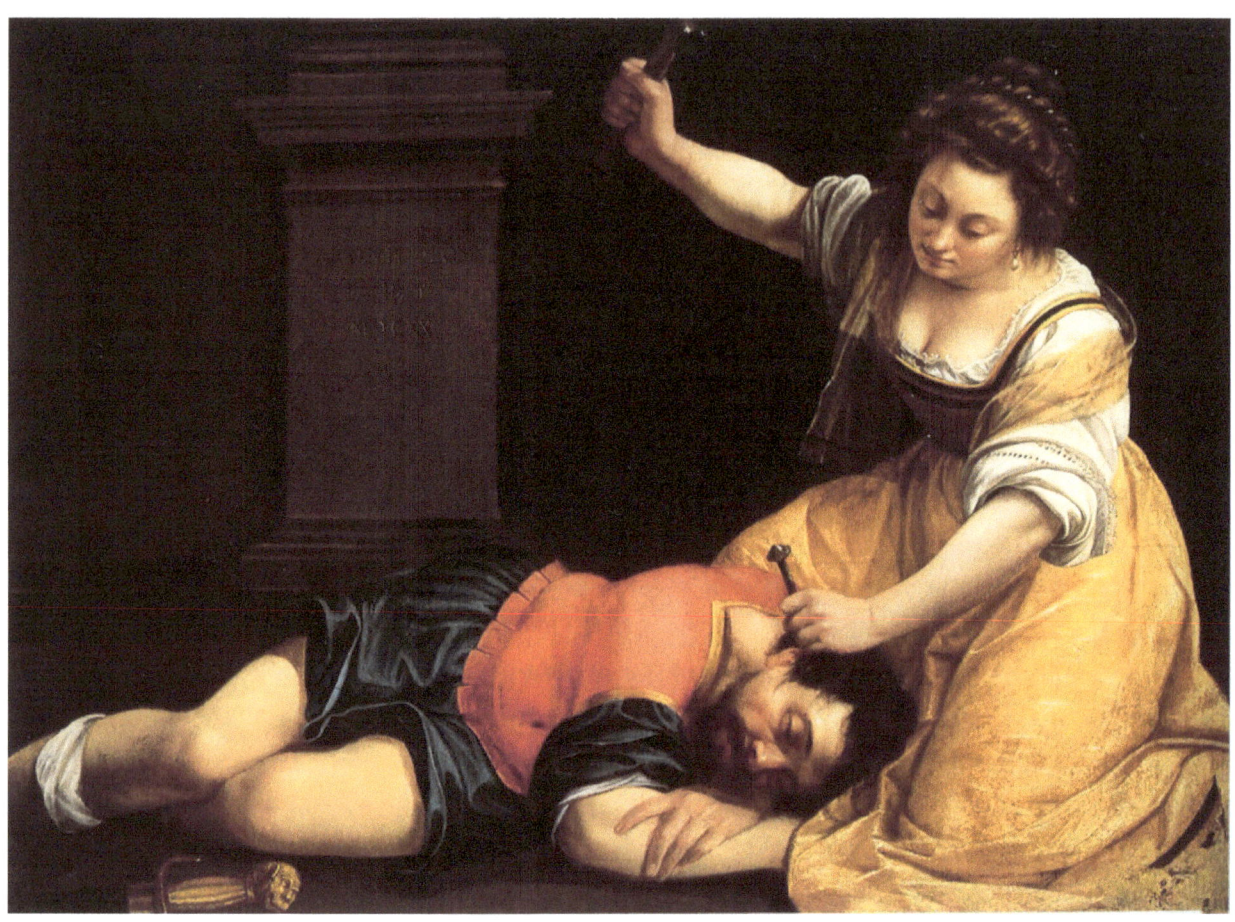

Jael and Sisera--1620

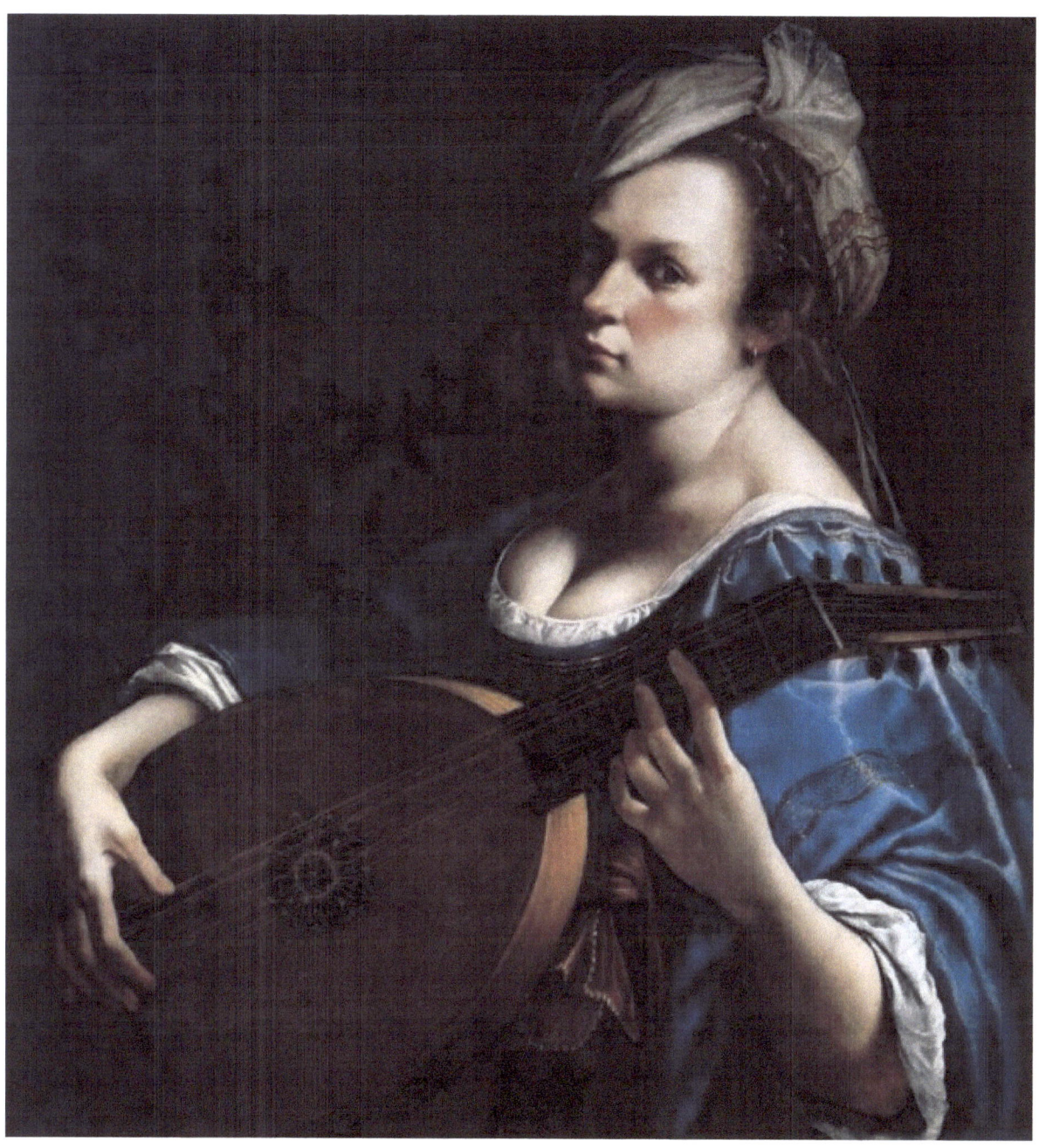

Artemisia Gentileschi - Self Portrait as a Lute Player

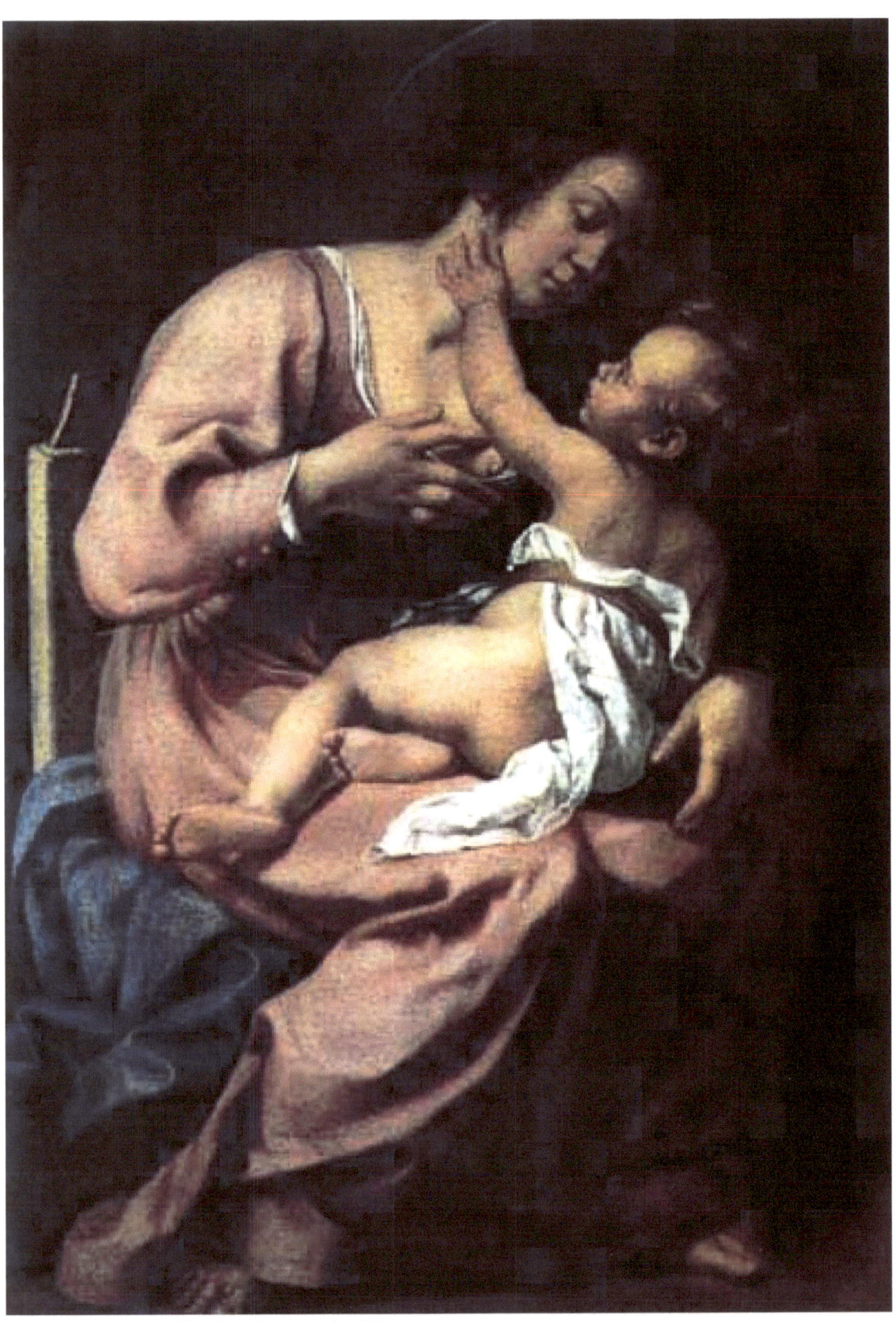

Madonna and Baby Jesus--1609

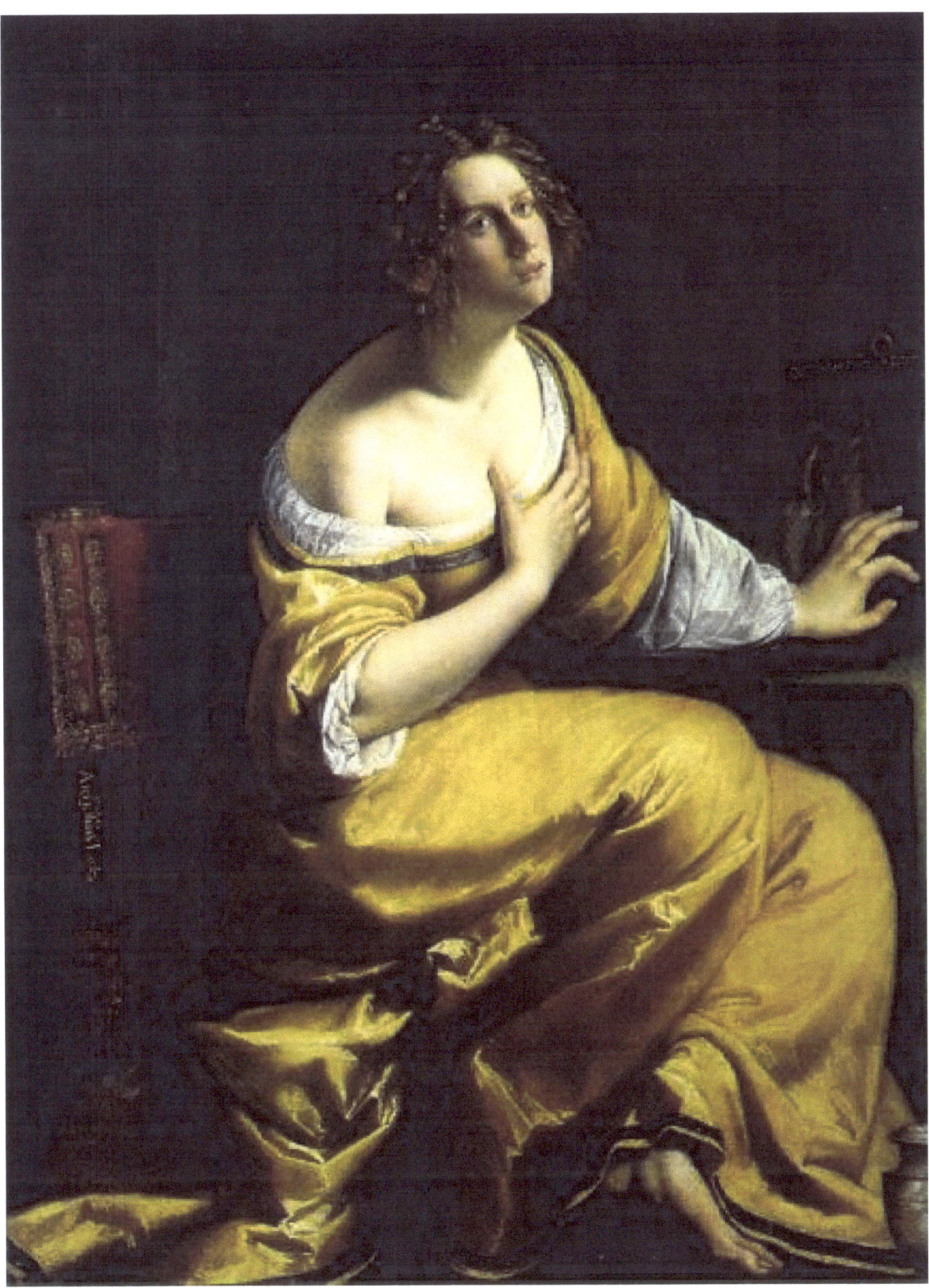

Mary Magdalen

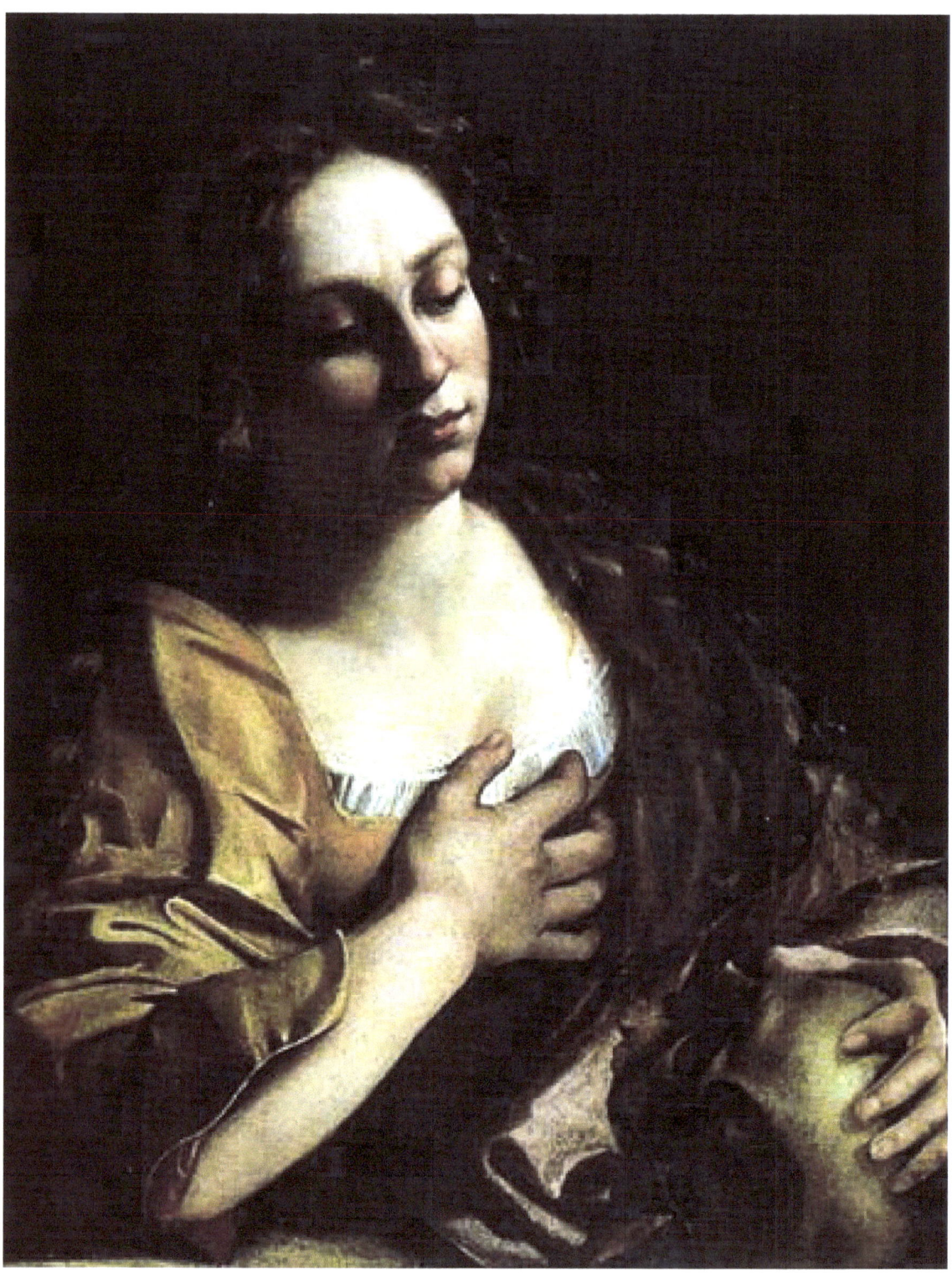

Penitent Magdalen-- Artemisia Gentileschi (?)

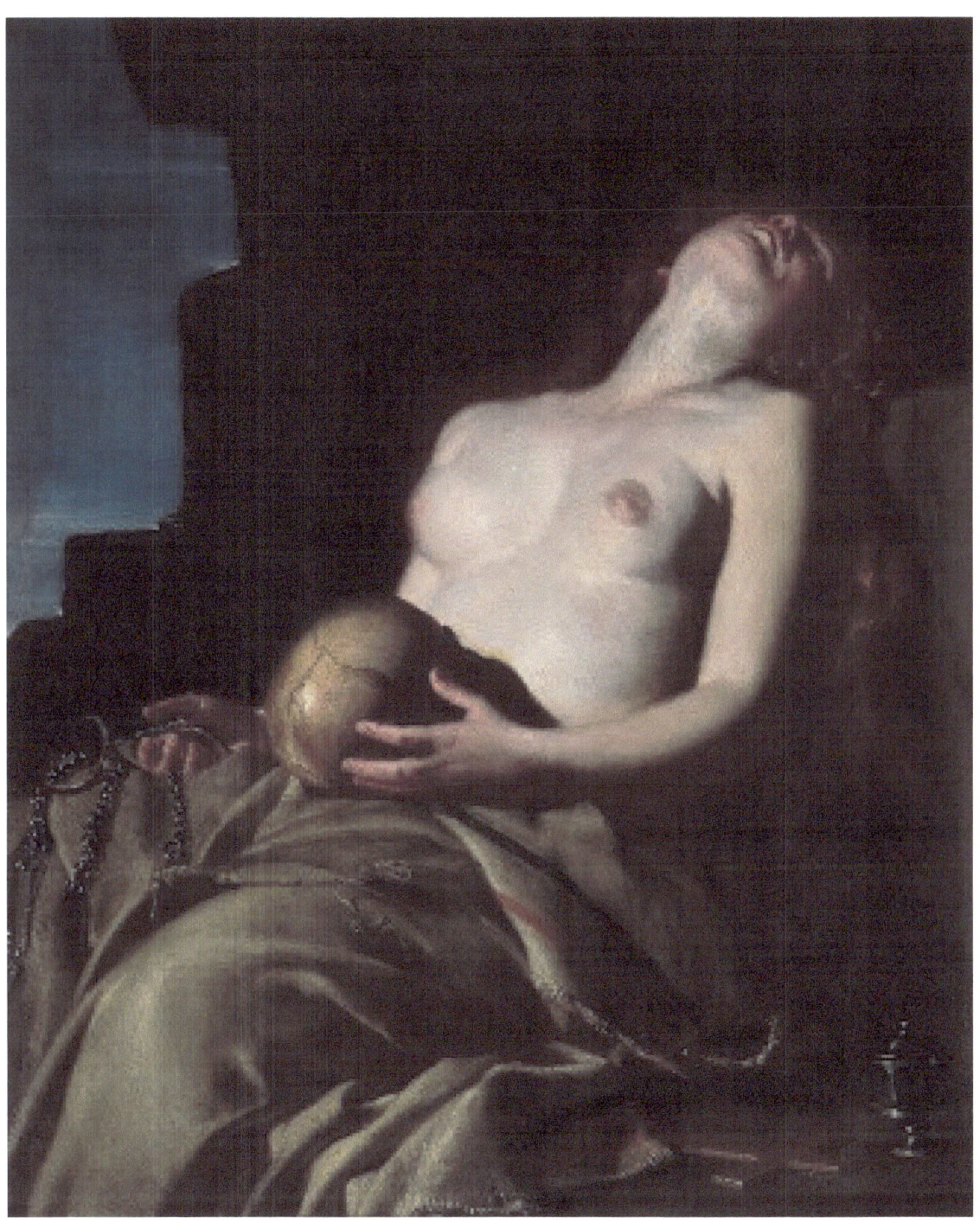

Madalena desmaiada

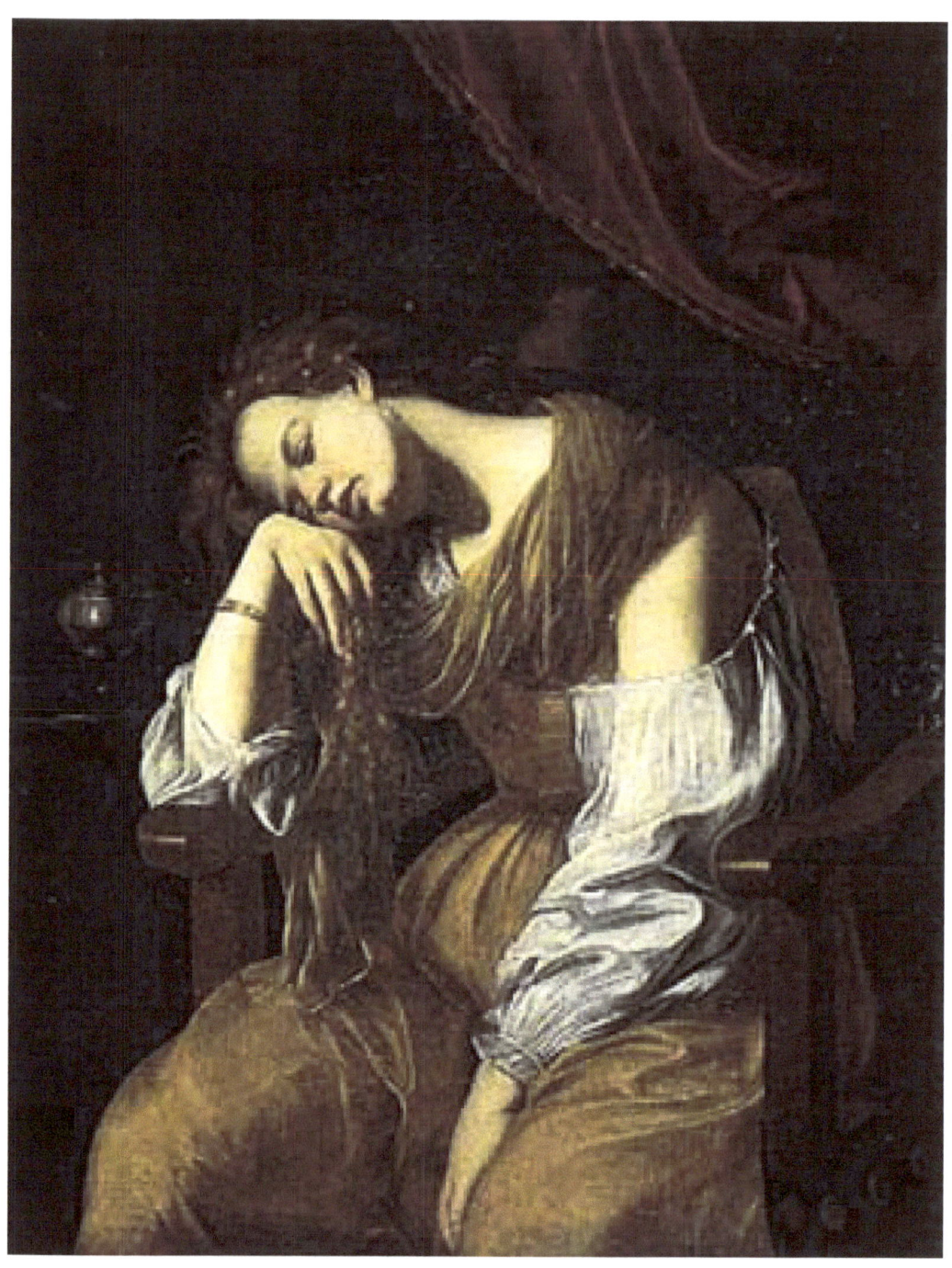

Mary Magalene as Melancholy 1621—1622

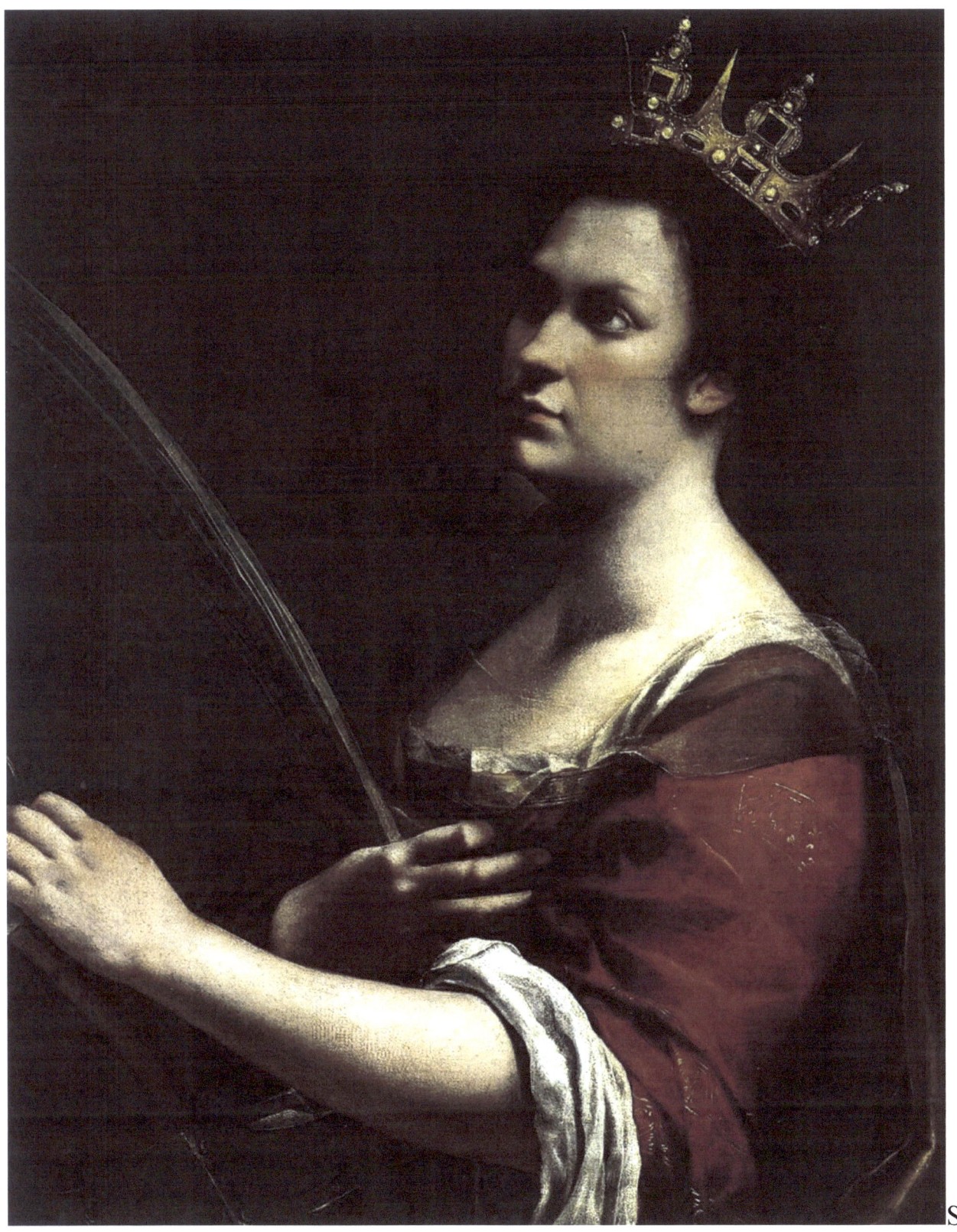

Catherine of Alexandria—1620

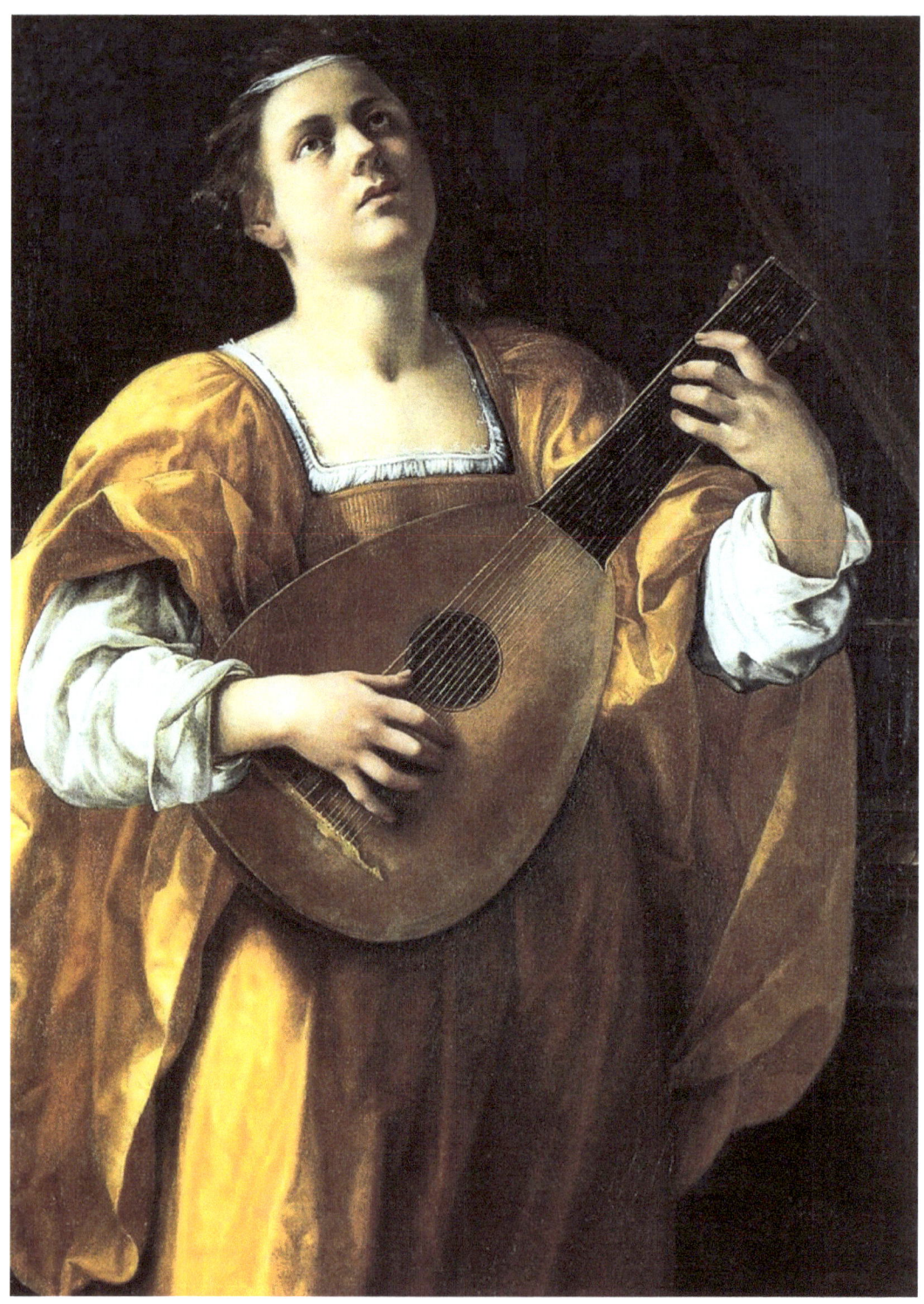

St Cecilia Playing a Lute—1616

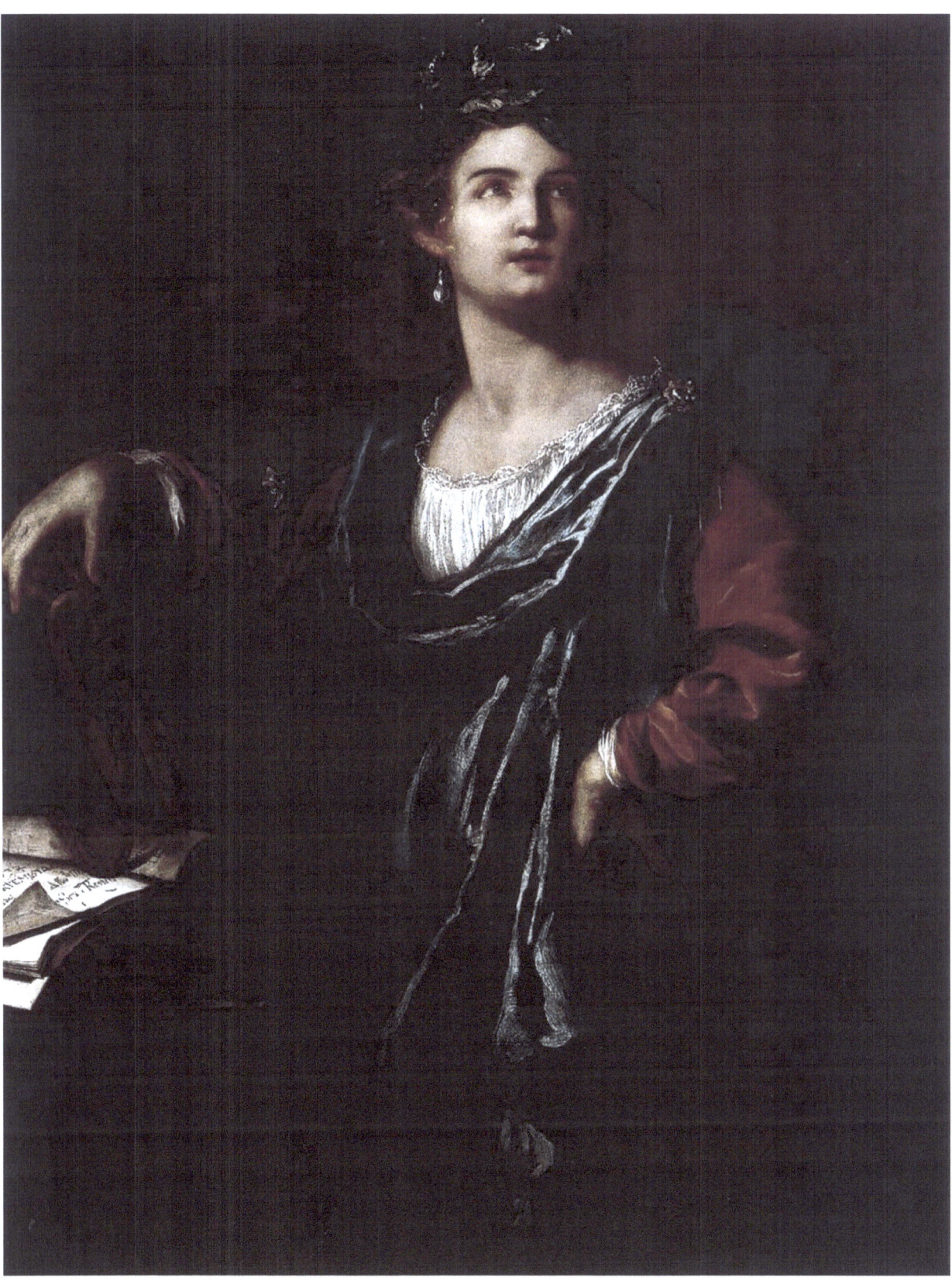

Clio, The Muse of History—1632

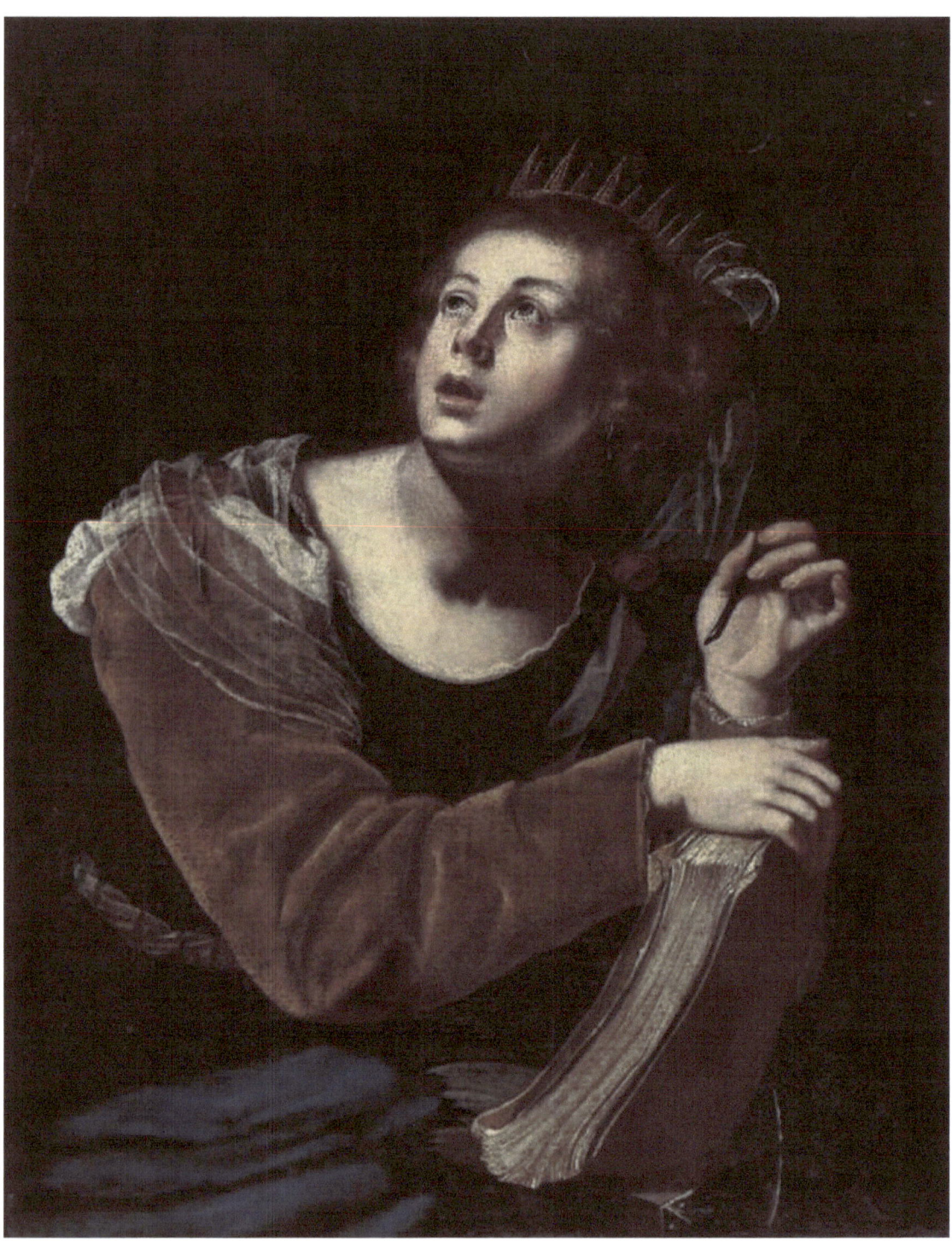

St Catherine of Alexandria

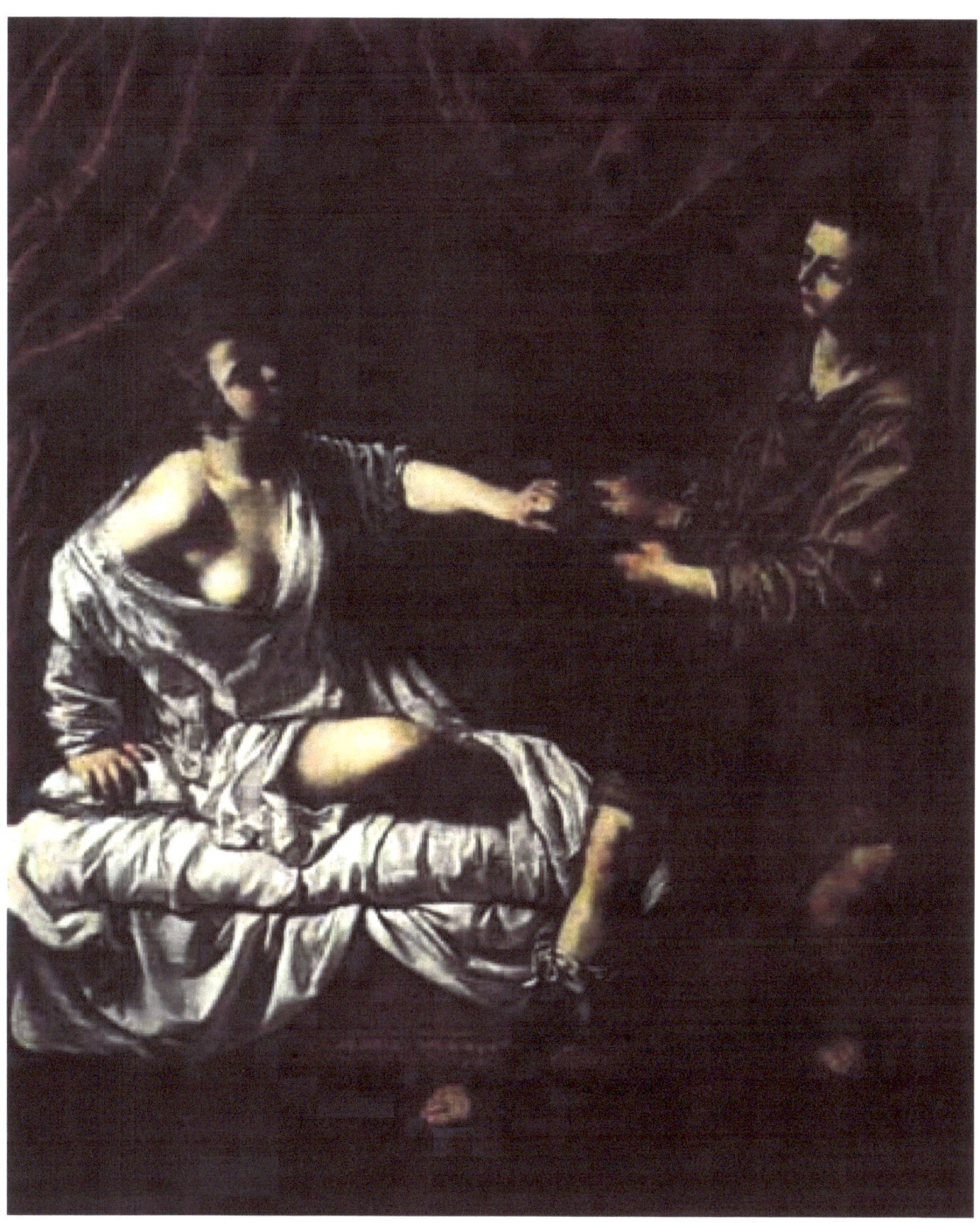

Joseph and Potiphar's-- Artemisia Gentileschi(?)

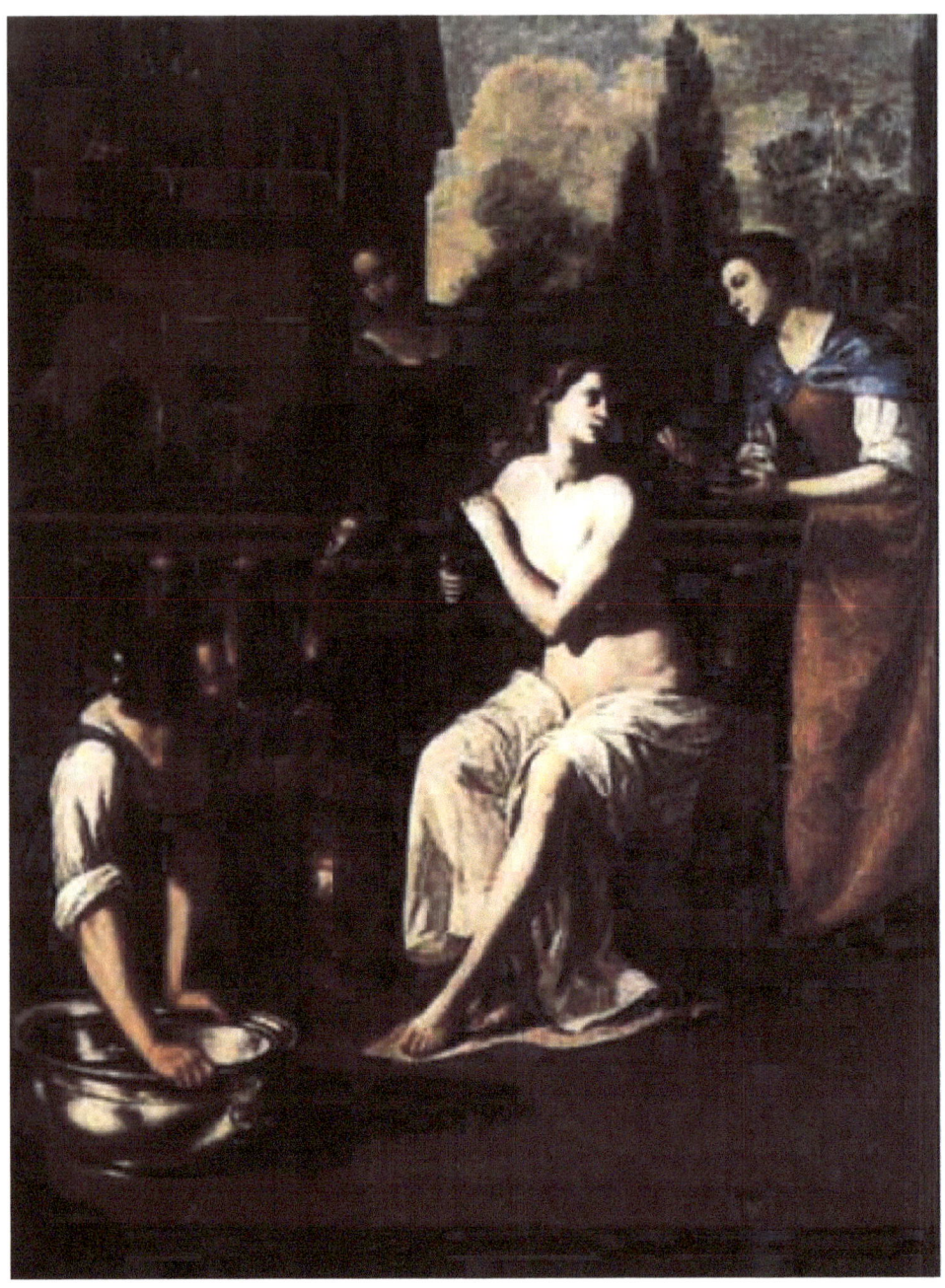

David and Bathsheba

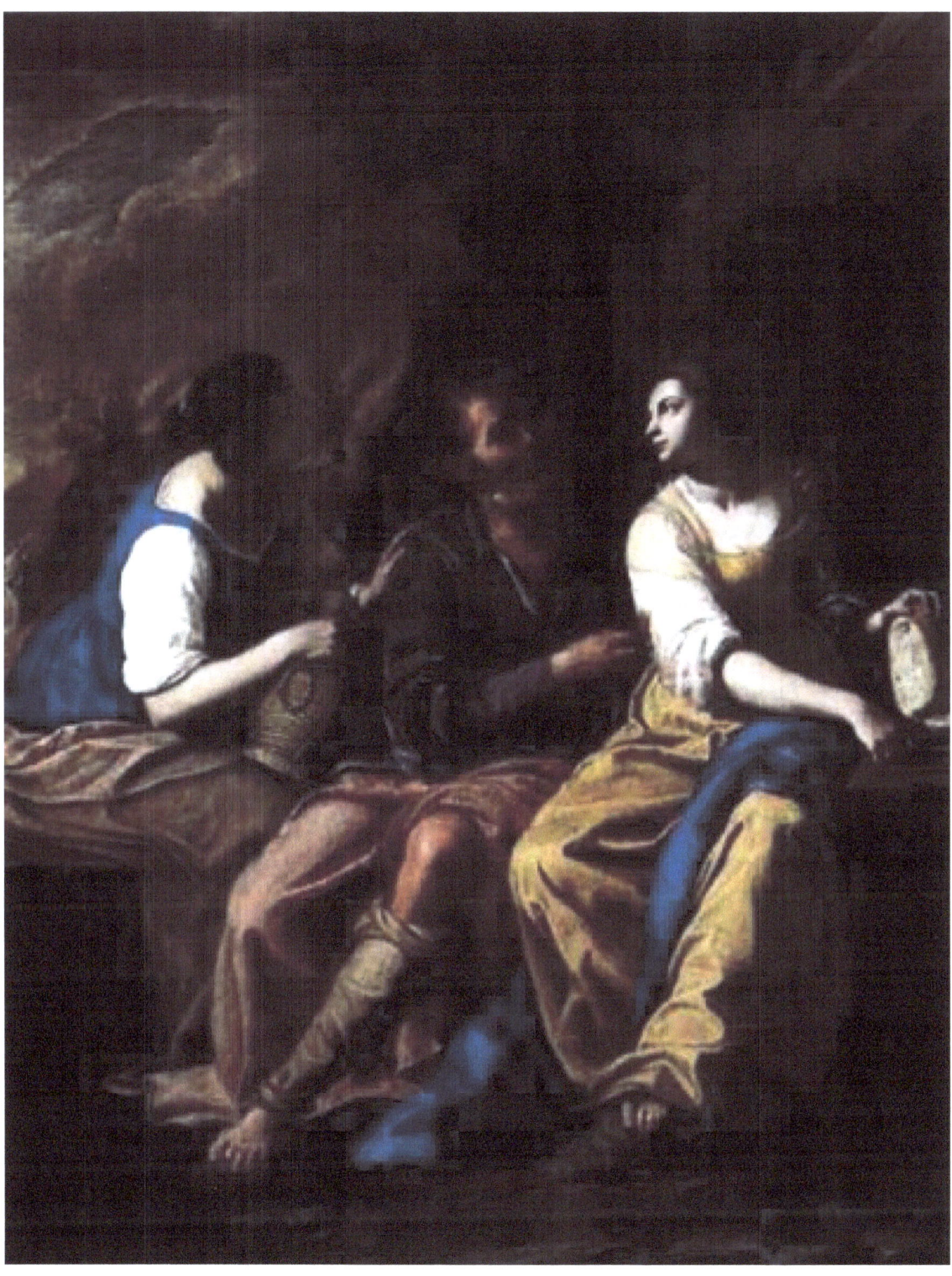

Lot and His Daughters

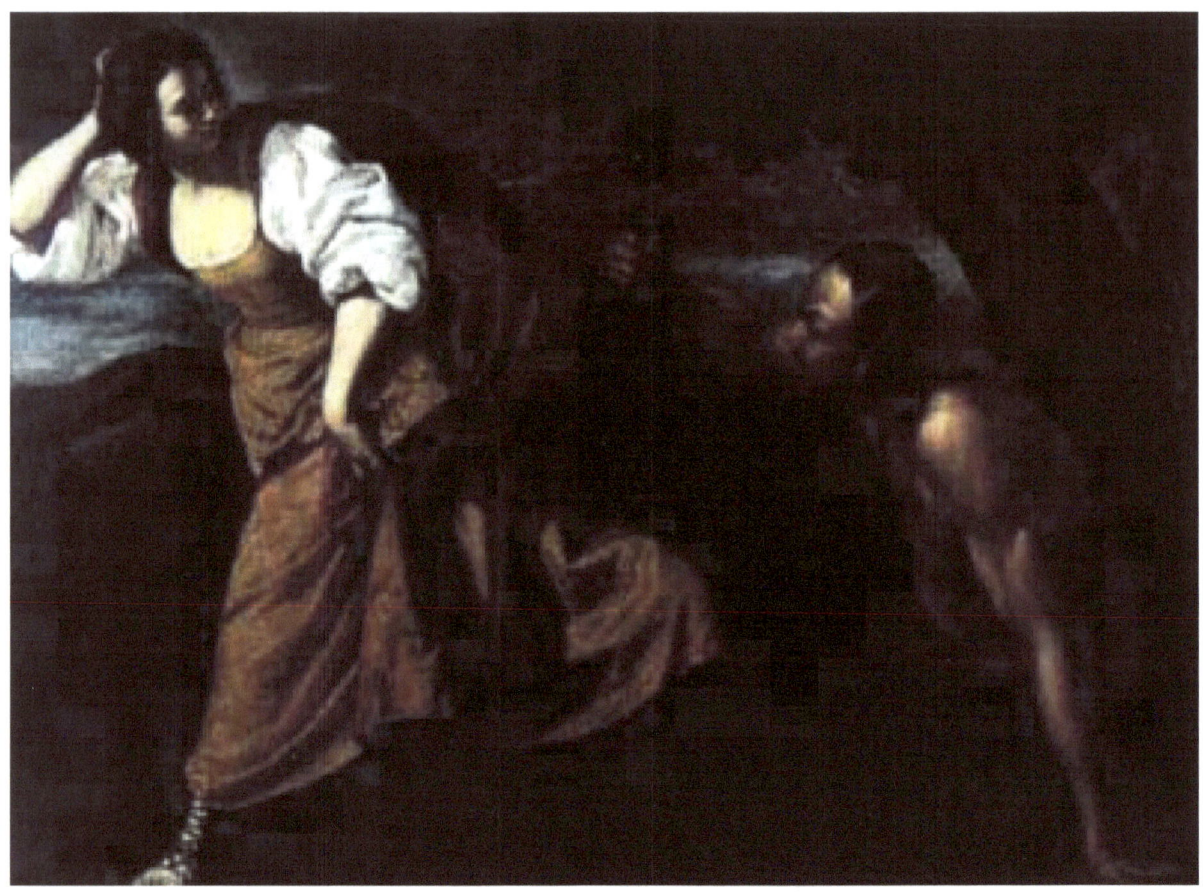

Corisca and the Satyr